D1389299

TRAVEL WRITING

PETER FERRY

• • •

TRAVEL
WRITING

Chatto & Windus
LONDON

Published by Chatto & Windus 2008

2 4 6 8 10 9 7 5 3 1

Chapters one and two appeared in a slightly altered form in *McSweeney's* #17 (2005);
"The Doctor", which is chapter two of book 2, appeared in slightly altered form in
the October 2004 issue of *New Review of Literature*; chapter eight of book 2 about
Quetico appeared in slightly altered form in the *Chicago Tribune* on 23 June 1985

While some characters in *Travel Writing* are real people, the book is a work
of fiction. The characters' words, actions and motivations are fictitious

First published in Great Britain in 2008 by
Chatto & Windus
The Random House Group Limited, 20 Vauxhall Bridge Road,
London, SW1V 2SA

www.rbooks.co.uk

Addresses for companies within The Random House Group
Limited can be found at: www.rbooks.co.uk/offices.htm

The Random House Group Limited Reg. No. 954009

A CIP catalogue record for this book
is available from the British Library

ISBN 9780701181925

The Random House Group Limited supports The Forest Stewardship Council
(FSC), the leading international forest certification organisation. All our titles that
are printed on Greenpeace approved FSC certified paper carry the FSC logo.
Our paper procurement policy can be found at:
www.rbooks.co.uk/environment

Mixed Sources
Product group from well-managed
forests and other controlled sources
www.fsc.org Cert no. TT-COC-2139
© 1996 Forest Stewardship Council

Designed by Linda Lockowitz

Printed and bound in Great Britain by
CPI Mackays, Chatham, ME5 8TD

For Lisa Kim,
Charlie Duke, and
Carolyn O'Connor Ferry

The men on the river were fishing. (Untrue; but then, so is most information.)

—E. M. Forster, *A Room with a View*

BOOK ONE
• • •

SOME TIME
AGO, WITH
CONTEMPORARY
INTERLUDES

1
• • •

TELLING STORIES

SOMETIMES I TRY to show my students the power of the story by telling them one. I say, "Last night I was driving home from work and—now, I'm just making this up off the top of my head—I noticed in my rearview mirror that there was a car swerving in and out of my lane. Anyway, I was on that stretch of Sheridan Road just south of Kenilworth that's two lanes each way and no divider and no shoulder and no margin for error, in other words, so I slowed down to let the car pass, or would have slowed down to let it pass me if this had really happened, which it didn't, and as it went by I had a look—a quick look—at the driver and I saw three things. First, that it was a woman and that she was very exotic and quite beautiful. Second, I noticed—or would have noticed if I weren't making this up—that there was something wrong with her; her head was bobbing as if she were drunk or sick or fighting sleep. Now, the third thing I noticed was that her shoulders were bare, and I had the strange sensation that more was bare—that her breasts were exposed or perhaps she was completely nude. Now, remember I'm just making this up. Anyway, I followed her for some time watching her weave and bounce off the curb, wondering what I should do, wishing I had a cell phone, although unsure who I would or should call, when we came to a red light and I found myself drawing up beside her."

By this point, a girl whose hair is green today and who has been passing notes is listening to me, and a dog-faced boy who has surreptitiously been doing his Spanish homework has stopped and a kid whose head was down on his arm— call him Nick—has sat up. When I have eye contact with each member of the class, I stop. I say, "But of course none of this ever really happened, and I've told you that four times, and you know it didn't happen. But look at you. You're interested, you want to know the rest, you want to know if she was naked and what was wrong with her and what I did or didn't do and all the rest, even though I'm making it all up right in front of you, and that is why stories are so powerful."

So, I'm a teacher, a high school teacher. In our society that gives me very little authority. About the highest compliment most people can pay a teacher is to ask why he or she became a teacher. That's supposed to be flattering, as in "You could have really done something important with your life." To boost my stock, I guess, I also do some writing, especially travel pieces for newspapers, magazines, and travel guides.

I teach English at the public high school in the wealthy Chicago suburb of Lake Forest, which in an odd way gives me even less authority than if I taught in a blue-collar neighborhood or a farm town where I would at least have more education than the parents of most of my students. In Lake Forest teachers are sometimes treated like the lawn service. "Honey, see if you have time to call the caterers about Saturday, and let's get someone out here to fix that toilet and someone to teach Charlie the difference between active and passive voice." Mind plumbers. But that's okay. It's a lovely place to teach, and we're paid a living wage. Besides, I like working with people who bring their own lunches and drive little cars. Most teachers are pretty good people.

Before teaching I worked for a publishing house. I sat in a windowless cubicle writing textbooks for which someone else made a lot of money; it isn't glamorous, but you can get rich if you can get every eighth grader in the state of Texas to read or at least buy your thirty-dollar book. And somehow people think that it *is* glamorous. I would go to parties and say I was an editor, and people, especially women—and that was important to me then—would say, "Oh, really?" and raise their eyebrows and look at me a little more carefully. I remember the first party I went to after I became a teacher, someone asked me what I did for a living, and I said, "Well, I teach high school." He looked over my shoulder, nodded his head, said, "I went to high school," and walked away.

Once I repeated that anecdote around a big table full of Mexican food in the garden at a place called La Choza in Chicago, and Becky Mueller, another teacher at the school, said that I was a "storyteller." I liked that. I was looking for something to be other than "just" a teacher, and "storyteller" felt about right. I am a teacher and a storyteller in that order.

I have made my living and my real contribution to my community as a teacher, and I have been very lucky to have found that calling, but all through the years I have entertained myself and occasionally other people by telling stories.

But it really did happen, of course, the girl in the car, or could have or might as well have happened. It happened just as surely as Ernest Hemingway went down to Pamplona with a bunch of people one of whom was not Lady Brett Ashley, but was Lady Duff Twysden, and she really did sleep with everyone under the sun so that years later when she died of tuberculosis at the age of forty-five in Taxco, Mexico, all of her pallbearers were former lovers, and they really did drop her casket coming down the steps of the cathedral, and those people all drank way too much and slept with each other or tried to and couldn't, so that one morning drinking coffee in the Café Iruña or six months later in Paris, Hemingway said "what if" and "suppose . . ." It happened just as surely as Stephen Crane was shipwrecked off the coast of Florida in 1896 and spent four days in a lifeboat and then wrote one of the best American short stories ever about it. But it hadn't happened the night before, and, of course, the woman wasn't naked; I just put that in for purposes of teenage titillation. No, it was some time ago now on a Friday evening in December a week or two before winter break. I had stayed around to clear my desk, so it was after six when I was driving home for the weekend, tired and happy. And she really *was* swerving crazily and bouncing off curbs. I did get behind her, and as she went by I had just a glimpse of her and saw that she was quite beautiful, although I must tell you that I have a thing about falling in love with women I see through glass. Once I had a fantasy that lasted some months about a drive-in bank teller with a sexy voice. I finally had to see who she was, so I went into the bank. From a distance I spotted her at the drive-in window with her back to me, and I was thrilled, but when she turned around I saw that she was horse faced and middle-aged. I went back to my car disappointed and wondering what I had fallen in love with and if I was still in love with it. So, anyway, I followed Lisa Kim, for that was her name, down Sheridan Road on this dark winter evening, which wasn't very hard because her right rear taillight cover was broken and the light shown white. I followed her, becoming increasingly fascinated and concerned at the same time. How had she gotten so drunk so early? Had she been to an office party? And what could I possibly do about this situation? I looked for a cop, or rather hoped one would see her because by the time I'd have told the story, she'd have been gone, lost in the traffic. Could I signal to her? Should I pull up beside her and have another look? But there was no doubt she was in trouble, and besides, she might swerve into my lane and drive me into oncoming traffic. And why was I so concerned? Would I have been if she had been a woman on a cell phone in an SUV? A black guy with his cap on sideways? An old man? Then there was the stoplight when I did pull up beside her, the one at Sheridan Road and Lake Street, the one just before the S curve that skirts the Baha'i temple. And there she was, head bobbing, car hazy with smoke, music so loud I could hear the words although both our windows were up. It was then that I could have done something. Over beers a few days later, a friend who is an attorney would say, "You'd have been in big trouble legally."

"But what about morally?"

"I don't know about that, but legally you'd have been in big trouble."

Moot point. I didn't do anything. Before I could decide what to do or if to do and just after she had looked at me and we had for one tiny, shadowy instant made eye contact and I had seen on her face a look that may have said "watch this" but may have said "do something," the light changed and she pulled away. Fast. She fishtailed and drove right through the S curve, missed it completely, hit the curb with her front tires hard, which launched her into the air, and hit a cast-iron lamppost about four feet off the ground, breaking the damn thing in half. I got there about the same time as a man in a camel-hair coat and a younger woman who might have been his wife. They had been coming north. We looked through the driver's window. Lisa Kim was lying facedown across the passenger seat and onto the floor. There was some blood, but not too much. I felt the door handle, pulled it carefully, tentatively, pulled the door open (it creaked but came), reached across, and turned off the engine, although my hand was shaking so badly that I could barely do it. Already there were sirens.

The young policeman said I shouldn't worry about it, that I couldn't have prevented it.

"But what if I'd blocked her at the light, taken her keys?"

"Then I'd probably be here arresting you."

"But she was driving drunk. I mean, look what happened."

"Yeah, I know, but there was nothing you could do, really."

"That's a little hard to accept." But I accepted it, at least in part, and began to feel a little better. And we all felt better when someone (the man in the camel-hair coat?) said he thought he saw her move on the gurney, and someone else (the younger woman who might have been his wife?) was sure she groaned.

"She'll be all right."

"Kids are tough. Kids are resilient."

That's the great thing about being American; we're so relentlessly cheerful and optimistic. Our glass is always half full. Daisy's green light is always out there giving us hope. I just don't believe that a group of Europeans would have reached the same conclusion that we did before we got back in our cars and went on about our lives.

I read somewhere that 60 percent of Americans still believe in Heaven and Hell. Of that 60 percent, 97 percent think that they personally will go to Heaven. Only 3 percent of that 60 percent or 1.8 percent of all Americans think they are going to Hell. Wouldn't that distress Cotton Mather? Wouldn't it make Norman Vincent Peale proud? I mean, talk about corn fed, Rocky Balboa, Little-Engine-That-Could positive thinking. Even the most basic understanding of human nature and the law of averages would suggest a miscalculation.

Lisa Kim was dead. Dead on Arrival. DOA.

I once heard Kurt Vonnegut say a writer has to believe that what he's writing right now is the most important thing anyone has ever written. That was hard for me in the beginning because my Presbyterian minister father taught me to be modest, humble, and circumspect. At potluck suppers in the church basement, we always waited to be the very last in line. I never learned how to be important.

Then along came David Lehman. In high school an English teacher told David that he was a poet, and he believed her. The day I met him he stuck his head out of his dorm-room door as I was entering mine for the first time, suitcases in hand (we were both students in a summer program at St. Hilda's College, Oxford) and asked me, "You don't have a copy of the *Paris Review* with you do you?"

"What?"

"The new *Paris Review*. I've got a poem in there. Hi. I'm David Lehman. I'm a poet." I did not see a poet. I saw a gawky, pimply eighteen-year-old kid with a New York accent and a Yogi Bear lilt in his voice.

"Pleased to meet you," I said. "Pete Ferry, Undersecretary of the Interior." David didn't seem to hear me. He shook my hand. Oh, we had a good time with David for a couple of weeks. We (three of us had come together from Ohio and had never even been to New York much less London) had chips on our shoulders, probably a bit of residual Midwestern adolescent anti-Semitism, and an absolute phobia about being ugly Americans. And now one of us was David, our worst fear, the ugliest American of all, a New York Jew. So we mocked him, imitated him, asked him stupid questions ("Do poets wear boxers or whitey-tighties?"), and it all missed him. ("I don't think it really matters. I wear briefs. Kenneth Koch wears boxers. This I happen to know because I once came home to my apartment to find him playing the violin in his boxers for a graduate student in comparative literature. She was quite beautiful.") For a couple of weeks we huddled together talking about all the stupid things David did and said, and then he did something stupider. He challenged John Fuller to a poetry reading. We were just mortified.

Fuller was one of our dons. He was young, handsome, witty, wry, bored, very British. He was also a rising star among British poets and the son of Roy Fuller, who was the sitting poet laureate of Oxford University. Fuller accepted, and on a Wednesday evening after sherry and shepherd's pie, we sat back gleefully to watch David's vivisection.

John Fuller began the evening with some nakedly deprecating remarks about his young challenger from across the sea. He was at least annoyed, perhaps insulted. We choked on our laughter, bit our thumbs, but David beamed at us oblivious, certain that we were all on his side or certain of something, at least. Then they began to read. They took turns standing at the podium. We were quieted. David wasn't that bad. David was pretty good. We looked sideways at each other and raised our eyebrows. After half an hour, David said that he would now read some of the New York poets who had influenced him: Koch, Frank O'Hara, David Shapiro.

"No, no," said Fuller with a wave of his hand. "Read your own stuff." They read on. David was damn good. After an hour, Fuller took the podium and looked back at David. "Got a long piece?"

"Well, no . . ."

"I have one long piece I want to read. If you have something, too, we'll read these and then go home."

"Well, I have one, but I'm still working on it."

"Try it. I want to hear it."

"Well, okay."

"You first," said John Fuller.

And David read a poem called "Supercargo." He shuffled pages and started quietly, perhaps uncertainly, but his voice rose and rose with the poem, and he stood forward on his toes although he was tall to begin with. He was wonderful. When he finally sat down, we found ourselves clapping.

Fuller took the podium and looked down for a long moment at his loose sheets. "I can't follow that," he said finally, and sat down, too. Oh, we had a party that night. The girls dangled their bare summer legs from our dorm windows over the Cherwell River, and we all laughed and sang and passed bottles of Spanish Graves. We toasted David all night long.

For the rest of the term, I spent as much time as I could with David Lehman. We ate Chinese food because David was homesick, hitchhiked to the seashore reciting poetry between rides and made plans to go to France, where David said "the vegetables all taste like fruits." Before the end of the summer, Fuller, who had a little basement press, had published a broadsheet of David's poetry (I still have a copy of it somewhere), and I knew I wanted to be a writer and was able to say it aloud, at least to myself.

On Saturday evening Lydia Greene and I met some pals at Davis Street Fish Market for dinner. It is the place we gather most frequently because it has good, inexpensive seafood and a wonderful oyster bar where we always start and often finish the evening (sometimes we never get into the dining room) with platters of oysters and clams, plates of calamari, bowls of mussels, peel-and-eat shrimp, red beans and rice, fresh sourdough bread, and lots of good beer and wine.

As always, Officer Lotts was the first one there. He had claimed our favorite table and was sipping a glass of pinot grigio while reading the *Times* and waiting for the rest of us. He is an unusual cop. A late child of middle-aged parents who took him around the world and gave him everything under the sun including a leafy suburban life, every album ever made, and a gleaming white convertible with tan leather interior when he was sixteen, Steve Lotts started saying at the age of four that he wanted to be a Chicago policeman. "Sure," people said, "good!" But he was still saying it when he went to college to study criminal justice, and still saying it after a year spent as a guard at a nuclear-power plant, two and a half as a paralegal, and four as an internal-affairs investigator when he was finally admitted to the police academy. Even then people were sure he would bail out and head for the suburbs, but today he is an undercover gang-crimes cop who is on the street every day and often night, and is one of the few people I know who truly loves his work. He lives in an apartment full of plants and cats, wears horn-rimmed glasses and a Little Lord Fauntleroy haircut, and attracts wistful, waifish women.

"Ride your bike?" I pulled out a stool.

"Yep." He pointed at it through the window locked to a parking meter.

"Armed?" I asked lifting up his backpack.

"Of course," he said. He rarely goes anywhere without his

gun. I had been waiting all week to talk about Lisa Kim, and I almost told Steve the story right then, but I knew I'd only have to repeat it later, so I didn't. It was difficult.

Pretty soon everyone was there, laughing, eating, telling stories. Carolyn O'Connor was dating a gastroenterologist from Terre Haute. He took her for a walk through the woods on a farm he owns in Brown County, and in a clearing they came upon a table set with white linen, candles, a lovely meal, glasses of wine already poured. "I have no idea how he did it." Carolyn smiled; she may have the best smile in the world.

Carolyn's family and mine have summer homes in the same Michigan beach resort, and I've always known her, although I grew up playing with her older brothers and sisters. Then when she moved to Chicago after law school and rented an apartment with Steve Lotts on Fargo Street two blocks from where Lydia and I were living, we started hanging out with them and with Wendy Spitz, too, a lawyer pal of Carolyn's from her law firm.

It was Wendy who turned to me that evening and said, "I read that piece of yours about you and Lydia in Mexico."

"Me too," said Carolyn, "and I have a question for you."

"Is it really that beautiful?" Wendy asked.

"'Course it is," I said. "Why would you ask that?"

"Well, you know, travel writers . . ."

"It's like paradise," said Lydia, at the same time pointing out that a lot of beautiful places are full of odd people.

"Like Charlie Duke," said Carolyn. "That was my question. Is he a real person?"

"Oh, he's real," said Lydia.

Wendy said, "What I want to know is is he gay? You never make it clear."

There ensued a rambling discussion of our friend Charlie, his sexuality, his drinking habits, the drinking habits of homosexuals, the definition of alcoholism, the trustworthiness of alcoholics, whether it's possible to be friends with an alcoholic, the nature of friendship, and the nature of love itself. None of this was of any interest to me, but I hadn't yet seen my opening into Lisa Kim. I crossed my arms and listened. I felt like a sniper lying in wait.

"But can you love someone you can't trust?" asked Wendy.

"Of course you can," said Carolyn. "Think about children; you love them but can't trust them. Even most teenagers. Even a lot of old people."

"In fact," I said, "some people can't love someone they *do* trust. They lose interest." I wondered as soon as I said it whether my statement had a subtext, and if it did, I wondered if Lydia had picked up on it.

I didn't look at her, but I heard her say, "I don't think that's real love."

"Oh, who the hell knows what real love is," I said quickly, flippantly.

"Quick, change the subject," said Lydia. "Don't get him started on love."

"Okay, what are we going to read about next, Pete?" asked someone.

"Thailand. I'm going to Thailand over Christmas." I told them I wanted to update the whole Europe-on-$5-a-day idea of the sixties. Thailand on $50 a day and then a bunch of other places in Asia and Latin America. "Gee, Pete," said Steve, "how did you ever think of that?"

"I don't suppose you got a free airfare out of this, did you?" asked someone else.

"Are you going, Lydia?" someone asked.

She rolled her eyes and shook her head. "I'm waiting for his series on extravagant vacations in ridiculously opulent places. This one's going to be overnight trains and bad noodle houses and youth hostels with no air conditioning."

By now we'd all had a couple of drinks. There was the briefest lull in the conversation, and I pulled the trigger. "I gotta tell you guys about this accident I saw." For the most part they listened attentively.

Afterwards Steve asked, "Did you have a cell phone?"

"No. I wish I did."

"So what do you think you could have done?" asked Carolyn.

"He thinks he could have gotten out, opened her door, turned her car off, and taken the keys," said Lydia. "That's what he thinks."

"Okay, even if you could have done all of that, what next?" asked Carolyn.

"What next? I'm not sure," I said.

She went on, "I mean, you're blocking traffic, both lanes. Are you going to drive her car? What about *your* car?"

"What if she jumps out and gets run over?" asked Wendy.

"You could be held responsible," said Officer Lotts. "You could have been arrested yourself."

"For what?"

"What if she started screaming?" asked someone.

"Harassment," said Steve. "Assault. Who knows? Maybe even kidnapping."

"But she was out of control! I mean, look what happened for crying out loud."

"Yes, but it wouldn't have happened if you'd stopped her." Wendy said that my only justification for interfering with the drunk girl was that it did happen, and if I'd interfered, it wouldn't have. No accident, no justification. She said I did the right thing, which was nothing.

"How could it be the right thing if I had it within my power to save someone's life, and I didn't do it?" I asked.

"But at what risk?" asked Steve. "Your own life, maybe? Our rule is that you act only to help someone else when you are sure that you are safe. Very first priority always is your own safety."

"How about the fireman who goes into a burning build-ing to rescue someone?"

"He doesn't. He really doesn't. Not unless he's damn sure and his supervisor's damn sure, too, that he can go in and get back safely. A supervisor would never let his people go in there under any other circumstance. It's rule number one. Secure yourself first. Now if the roof caves in or the building collapses, that's a different story, but you don't know that it's going to happen."

"See, I think that's Pete's problem," said Carolyn. "He knew what was going to happen. You know what I mean? He could see it happen before it happened, and then it hap-pened." (Of course I now know that even if for a moment I could see what was going to happen to Lisa Kim, I had no idea what had already happened to her and would not for a long time.)

"It's almost like a tree falling in the woods," said Wendy.

"Or like Pandora's box." Carolyn said that knowledge of the future was the one thing that didn't get out of Pandora's box, and for a moment I had it and was therefore very briefly Godlike. She also said that since I'm Pete Ferry and not God, I wanted to do something human, like fix things.

"I thought it was hope that didn't get out," said someone.

"Okay," I said, "I've got a legal question."

"No legal questions!" Wendy threw up her hands. "We're off duty. No free legal advice. Besides, I'm quitting. I'm done with the law."

We all moaned. We'd heard this many times.

"I'm done making rich people richer. I'm sick of this corporate shit. I'm going to do something that matters with my life." Wendy was off to the races about how she was going to collect her bonus and resign her partnership, sell her condo, see the world, run a marathon, learn Spanish, get an MBA, and move to South America. "Within five years I intend to be the finance minister of a small country somewhere in Latin America!"

"*Ándale!*" someone said.

"I'm going to finally do something fucking important with my life!"

"*Arriba!*" we cried. By this time the waitstaff was eyeing us wearily. Later that night I lay awake in bed thinking about doing something important with my life. I was aware even then that something in me had changed. I was not sure what it was or how big it was or how long it would last, but something was different. I had seen another person die. I thought about soldiers who can never quite come all the way back from combat, can never really shop again for tube socks at Wal-Mart or go all out for a foul pop-up or fall asleep on the couch with a book turned over on their chests. Can never even read a book or eat soup or make love without the knowledge of what they've done or seen.

For me right then, it was the knowledge of what I hadn't done. Oh, I knew that my friends were well-meaning, that they were kind and wise and generous to reassure me and I was sure they were right that any action I would have taken could have failed or backfired or even exacerbated the situation, but they were also missing the point. I saw someone alive, and then I saw her dead, and in between I could have acted at least theoretically, at least hypothetically, to change the dynamic between those two things. Perhaps that's what had changed. Perhaps I'd never realized before that I could have such power. Perhaps I'd never even thought about it.

The first real writing I ever did was a bunch of short stories I wrote as a senior thesis at Ohio University for Walter Tevis, and I had been carrying around something that Tevis had said to me ever since, something that despite the fact that I'd spent much of my life writing made me hesitate to call myself a writer.

I would love to say that Walter Tevis was my mentor, but it would be more accurate to say that I wanted him to be my mentor, and he tried to be, sort of. I don't think that I was very mentorable because I was only playing at being a writer, trying it on as you might a suit of clothes, and I think he knew that, but he was kind and indulgent and treated me as a mentee even if we both knew we were faking it.

Tevis was a goofy, gangly, buck-toothed man who knew Paul Newman and drank wine, sometimes too much. I'm not telling tales out of school here; he was candid about his drinking and used to joke that the only day of the year he didn't drink was New Year's Eve, "amateur night," and every New Year's Day he gave a brunch so he could enjoy his bleary-eyed friends and welcome the new year with a Bloody Mary. About Paul Newman: He had supposedly and very briefly—if at all—attended Ohio University, and we as undergrads were much more impressed that Tevis knew him than that the reason he knew him was because he had written two novels called *The Hustler* and *The Color of Money* that had been made into movies starring Newman. This all made Tevis something of a local celebrity, and I considered myself lucky to get into his creative-writing class as a junior and luckier still when he agreed, somewhat reluctantly, to sponsor my independent-writing project the year I came back from Oxford.

I spent the winter quarter sitting up all night in my tiny room smoking cigarettes, drinking Nescafé and typing five rambling, mediocre stories about growing up. Once a week Tevis and I met late in the evening. The hour was partly because we were both night owls and partly, I came to realize, so Tevis would have a reason to open a bottle of Spanish sauterne that was sometimes not his first. We met in his living room at first, but his wife, who had correctly assessed the situation and clearly saw me as a bad influence and facilitator, would walk through glowering at us, so we moved our sessions to the detached garage Tevis had remodeled into a study. It was a small space, and we spent much of our time there avoiding eye contact. I was like that person you know who acquires a friend or girlfriend or wife or even a child because someone else has said that he should, who does and says all the right things, but who is only painting by numbers. We sat there time after time on the outside chance that Tevis might say one day, "He was my student," and I might say one day, "He taught me everything I know." But that is much too cynical. Actually, he taught me three very important things:

(1) He taught me about San Miguel de Allende, a lovely colonial town on the high plateau about three hours north of Mexico City that has a good school of art and one of music, some satellite-language schools, a handsome cathedral on a perfect little plaza, cobblestone streets, cheap inns and posadas, an English-language bookstore, and enough—but not quite too many—Americans. Tevis had gone to San Miguel on the advance he had gotten to write *The Hustler* and had spent most of his time there filling a drawer with *osos negros,* the little, black plastic bears that came chained to the necks of vodka bottles. I went there more recently to sit in the sunshine and to write down a good part of this story that you're reading.

(2) Tevis also taught me something valuable about the parts and importance of culture, our culture. At the time I knew him, he was busy suing a man named Rudolph Wanderone, whom he claimed had stolen his most valuable creation. One Sunday afternoon on a porch swing in Lexington, Kentucky, while he waited to be called for dinner, Tevis had invented a character out of whole cloth named Minnesota Fats, who would become the universal prototype of the pool

hustler. According to Tevis, Wanderone had come along and appropriated the name, and was making lots of money appearing on television as Minnesota Fats. Tevis was spending lots of money trying to prove that Rudolph Wanderone was Rudolph Wanderone. Since it seemed to be a losing battle, I asked him why he was doing it. For once, he answered me seriously. He said, "Pete, I've written a few good stories, but I'm not William Faulkner. No one is going to remember my stuff in a hundred years. But every school kid and every old lady in America knows who Minnesota Fats is. He's mine. I invented him. He's my little contribution to Americana, and I don't want that taken away from me."

"My goodness," I thought then and think now, "how wonderful to have given the rest of us Minnesota Fats or the Yellow Brick Road or Kraft marshmallow miniatures. You don't have to discover penicillin or win the Nobel Peace Prize or write *Hamlet*. It is enough to have thought up banana fish or invented a 'friend called Piggy.'"

(3) But that brings me to the third thing that I learned from Tevis: something about myself. It was a very specific thing tied to a very specific moment, a kind of revelation. We were sitting as usual late at night in Tevis's little study, and I was trying to sound glib and literary about my stories. Tevis was trying to seem interested. He leaned forward from his chair across the coffee table for the bottle of sauterne, lost his balance, and allowed himself to slowly topple onto the floor at my feet. I was horrified. He was unabashed. I sat primly, knees together like the pastor's wife. He rolled onto his back and looked at the ceiling. "Pete," he said, "I know that growing up is hard, I really do, but growing old is awful." He didn't

stir, but after a while he said, "I like what you are doing, I really do. I think you are sincere, and I think you are talented. You haven't much to say, but you say it very well."

I suppose that ever since, I've been looking for something to say. Along the way I've done a good bit of writing. Early on I wrote a defiantly plotless novel, got a kind and encouraging rejection letter from a young editor at Alfred Knopf, and published some of its chapters as short stories. I wrote a few other self-consciously literary short stories and even won an award for one. But mostly what I've written has been practical, utilitarian stuff, stuff that speaks for itself. I wrote textbooks, of course, and grant and award applications. I wrote a glossy sixteen-page brochure promoting a $31 million school-building referendum that passed by a mere 400 votes and for which I secretly took almost-complete credit. Lots of other people took almost-complete credit, too, but the thing did win some kind of national award; I have the plaque in my classroom. And over the years I have done a good bit of very subjective, highly personalized travel writing because I became interested in what we do and where we go to give our lives meaning when we don't or can't find it at home, when life there becomes too staid and certain and we have to create challenges—even dilemmas—for ourselves because problems are interesting and important and life without them is neither. It is the reason that people join the circus, I think, drink too much, drive too fast, jump off things, jump into things, climb things, run away from home, and paddle into the wilderness. It is also the reason they tell stories.

2

• • •

LYDIA AND LISA

Now, I need to tell you about Lydia Greene. This is, of course, my version of the story. There was a time when I thought it was our version, that she would have told you the same story, and up to a certain point in time, she might have.

Lydia Greene worked at an ad agency with my old high school friend Tom MacMillan, and after college I hung out some with them and a bunch of other agency people. One beery Friday night the three of us discovered that we were all looking for apartments, and by the end of a very long evening at some after-hours bar on the Near North Side feeling confidential, even intimate, in that way that you only can when you're drunk—I was able to see the other two only by closing one eye—someone was saying, "Listen, guys, each of us needs a bedroom, right?"

"Right."

"Right."

"But each of us doesn't need a living room, right?"

"Right."

"And we don't each need a kitchen or a bathroom, right?"

"Right."

"Or dining rooms?"

"Right."

"So why rent twelve rooms when what we really need is six? Let's go in together and get one of those great big three-bedroom places with hardwood floors and high ceilings and bay windows."

"I don't care."

"Whatever." There was a senior account executive at the ad agency where Lydia worked who called her and the other young art directors and copywriters "the whatever kids." He did a very amusing, shoulder-shrugging impersonation of their studied nonchalance and claimed that they had managed to transform a relative pronoun into a "bon mot that distilled four thousand years of Western cynicism and Eastern mysticism into a single word of which virtually every user is oblivious to origin, meaning, and implication."

So the three of us rented an apartment in Rogers Park, a neighborhood that couldn't decide if it was going up or going down, but was still close enough to the middle for our purposes. Our hardwood floors had paint speckles, but the place was big and airy with a little balcony and, if you stuck your head out far enough, a lake view. The night we moved in was another beery one, and this time Lydia and I discovered we were both liberals, baseball fans, and movie buffs, and ended up in the same bed. First thing she said in the morning was, "That was a mistake." When I mumbled a protest, she said, "Look, I need an apartment more than I need a boyfriend." We didn't mention that night again for a long time.

Then after two years, Tom fell in love and moved in with his girlfriend, and Lydia and I could neither afford the place without him nor find a suitable replacement. Still, we worked well together because we were both neat, quiet, and independent.

"Want to find an inexpensive two-bedroom, then?" I asked.

"Why not?"

Instead we found an expensive one-bedroom, but it was very cool. It was on Lake Michigan, all windows and light and French doors. There were only four rooms, but they were huge.

"One of us could sleep on the pullout in the living room," she said.

"Not me."

"Not me."

"Well, we could get twin beds," I said.

"Rob and Laura. Ugh."

"Well," I said. We looked at each other. "I guess we could sleep together."

We looked at each other some more. She shrugged. "Whatever. We did once. It wasn't so bad."

So that was that. Why not? At first we pretended to be roommates. Just roommates. But people would glance in our bedroom and raise their eyebrows. So then we decided to be lovers, but people would say, "Why isn't Lydia going with you to the wedding? To your parents for Thanksgiving? To Ecuador?" So finally we decided we were inventing an entirely new, completely unique kind of relationship. Lydia liked that idea a lot at the time. She had a kind of attitude, one that she had gotten at Bennington or perhaps earlier, about the whole falling-in-love-getting-married-and-growing-old-together thing. She called it an "unfortunate sentimental narrative," and while I didn't think this attitude was quite as original as she did, I accepted it and even adopted it sometimes. I did so as a matter of personal convenience. In truth, I thought then that there was something missing in her or me or between the two of us, something that could be defined only by its absence. At the same time, I suspected that that something was missing in everyone and that tales of love and devotion were either delusion or romance.

And, to be fair, there was a lot between Lydia and me. We liked some of the same things: mystery novels, foreign movies, hot food, cooking, Scrabble, Django Reinhardt, jigsaw puzzles, and dogs (we eventually got a big black-and-white pound dog named Art) in addition to baseball and later Mexico. And I liked her. I liked living with her. So we gave each other companionship, sex-when-it-suited-both-our-needs-but-never-otherwise-mister, respect, care, concern, even affection up to a point, and freedom. Lots of freedom.

At first we could see other people, and we were free to travel separately. In fact, we were free to go anywhere at any time with anyone for any reason, no questions asked. Lydia once disappeared for nearly a month, and only the fact that she seemed to have taken some clothing kept me from calling her parents or the police. When she finally showed up, she looked three years older, and I never did find out where she had been. We were definitely "don't ask, don't tell," and never, never require, request, insist, or report. Even a question as neutral and innocuous as "What time are you getting home from work tonight?" was forbidden. At first.

Seeing other people worked just fine until I brought one home.

"Where'd you pick *her* up?" Lydia asked the next day.

"Who?"

"That slut you were boffing in the living room last night."

"What? Why would you ever say something like that?" But we both knew, although neither of us could even quite think the word: jealousy. How horribly ordinary. In time our relationship became exclusive without either of us ever saying so, and in the end it became conventional. That was unfortunate because I would later realize that the main thing it had had going for it was that it wasn't conventional.

"Do you know," Lydia said one day, "that in the eyes of the state of Illinois, we are married?"

"Really?" I said.

"That's what someone told me. Common-law marriage. If you cohabit for five years, you have a common-law marriage."

"No kidding."

That was about the time we decided to go to Mexico to live for a while, and it may even have been the reason, or one of them. It's true that I was sick of corporate publishing and wanted to try to write that novel I mentioned, and Lydia was sick of the advertising business and wanted to try to paint, and it's true that Mexico was a very inexpensive place to live, but it's also true that Lydia and I were very much afraid of being like everyone else.

"What happened to that story?" asks the dog-faced boy.

"What story?"

"You know, the one about the dead girl. The girl in the car. Is it over?"

"Oh, *that* story. No, it's not over."

"But you keep going off on tangents," says the girl whose hair is green this day. "Can't you just tell us what happened?"

"I am."

"No, just to her. We don't want to hear about everything you ever wrote in your whole life or some dumb town in Mexico and all that crap."

"But that's all part of the story. The woman in the car is just another part."

"Can't you just tell us that part?" asks Nick.

"Okay. Here comes some more."

Evanston Weekly   *Thursday, December 14*

SHERIDAN ROAD CRASH FATAL

A Chicago woman was killed Friday evening in a one-car crash on Sheridan Road in Wilmette. Lisa Kim, age 28, was driving south near Gillson Park when her car left the pavement and hit a lamppost. Kim was pronounced dead on arrival at Evanston Hospital at 7:12 P.M. She was the only passenger in the vehicle.

Kim of 1854 N. Wolcott was a native of Kenilworth and a graduate of New Trier High School. She attended Northwestern School of Drama and was an original cast member of the musical review *Gangbusters*. She appeared in several local productions and the films *After the Opera* and *Oops!* She also made radio and television commercials and was employed at Trattoria Lemongello in Chicago.

Kim is survived by her parents, Dr. Roh Dae Kim and Dr. Pae Pok Kim, and three sisters: Maud Nho of Glenview, Sophie McCracken of Newport Beach, California, and Tanya Kim of Evanston. Funeral arrangements are being made with the Stanton Funeral Home in Kenilworth.

Attended Northwestern; didn't graduate. Original-cast member, but didn't go with the show to New York. 1854 N. Wolcott. Wicker Park or maybe Buck Town, certainly not Lincoln Park. The trattoria; still waiting tables? Four girls. I'll bet she was the second and the one in Glenview was the first. First-generation parents, second-generation kids. The one in California got away. Married a non-Korean. Doctor and doctor. I wanted to guess they were both pediatricians.

Another person I encountered along the way besides Walter Tevis who had something to say was one of my dermatologists, although I had no idea what he meant when he said it and have forgotten much of it since. Still, somehow I knew it was important, and as if to prove to myself that the fourth dimension is indeed time, I stuck some of it away somewhere until I was ready for it.

I had more than one dermatologist because I had very bad pimples. I don't remember where I found this doctor. I don't even remember his name for sure; I think it was Lorenz, but it may be been Lazaar. He seemed about seventy, had a potato face, smiling eyes, a tuft or two of hair, an Eastern European accent, and was Jewish, I think; his little office was at Devon and California, then the heart of the Jewish community in Chicago. I sat on the examining table and he on the little stool. I talked earnestly about my pimples and everything I'd tried with them, how they were interfering with my social life, and how now my hair was beginning to fall out; I probably went on and on. He responded by telling me this story that I don't remember very well, that at the time seemed a non sequitur. I don't think it was original. It had the sound of a parable, and I might even be able to find it somewhere if I looked, but I prefer my imperfect memory of it. It had to do with a young man, a Candide-like figure, who faced a series of travails in his life: illnesses, accidents, wars, catastrophes. And with each my little dermatologist would pause, raise his hands, and repeat the same refrain, which was something like, "So, it either kills you or it doesn't kill you; and if it kills you, you have nothing more to worry about, and if it doesn't, you go on."

I remember afterward going into the pharmacy in the building where a nervous, gaunt woman was trying to fill a prescription, and the pharmacist was abrupt with her, sent her away, looked over his glasses at me, and said, "Percodan addict." I realized that for the second time in an hour and perhaps for the first two times in my life, adults had taken me into their confidence, if in very different ways. I remember walking out into the hot sun full of feelings. Should I have been insulted by the doctor's story? Yes, my little problems had been dismissed, if gently, but somehow I felt flattered. Why did I think that he didn't tell this story to everyone? I was a little ashamed when I began to put two and two together: Devon Avenue, his accent, his age. If he hadn't been in a concentration camp himself, certainly he knew people who had. And here was this whiny American kid seeking medical attention because he wasn't getting laid enough. Or maybe those thoughts came only later, came after the story had settled deep into me somewhere, nested and fermented. Maybe that day I was just insulted and a little pissed off that he didn't understand just how tough it was to be pimple-faced and balding at the age of twenty. Yes, that's how it was. At any rate, I went on, but, of course, Lisa Kim did not, and here are ten possible reasons why:

(1) She was genetically predisposed to risk taking.

(2) She was still practicing adolescent rebellion.

(3) She was always practicing second-generation rebellion.

(4) A guy with whom she was in love had broken her heart recently.

(5) She'd had a late lunch with him that very day, and it hadn't gone well. She'd had two glasses of white wine.

(6) Because she was hurt and angry and because of the two glasses of afternoon wine, she'd gone to a Christmas party she had no intention of attending with people she knew better than to be around.

(7) One of them, a guy named Randy who was trying to get into her pants, gave her a joint, hoping she would smoke it with him. She didn't. She smoked it in the car on the way back to see the man who had broken her heart one more time.

(8) Two of the people at the party bought rounds of shooters at the same time just as Lisa was leaving, and she drank both shots straight down.

(9) None of the people at the party said, "Hey, Lisa, you shouldn't be driving."

(10) I didn't open her door, reach across her, and take her keys.

Now, obviously I was at the end of a rather long list, my involvement being both very late and relatively incidental. Still, had I stopped her, she would have gone on a while longer: an hour, a day, a year, a lifetime. And just maybe someday she'd be telling someone about that night, laughing in embarrassment. "Jeez, I was so trashed, some absolute stranger pulled me over and took my keys. Can you imagine? Man, was I lucky." Instead, her life was over and my life was somehow different.

Now I'm going to try again telling you about the funeral. I've tried before, but without success. It came out sounding like bad situation comedy what with the mistaken identity, incorrect assumptions, and people finishing each other's sentences. Cheap laughs, but it really wasn't like that at all.

I had to go, of course, although I didn't mention it to Lydia; it had turned out that she had little patience with my interest in Lisa Kim.

Outside the door were two knots of friends: the old suburban, high-school friends in their casually expensive, saggy, baggy just-so clothes and the urban theater friends in their tighter, blacker, angrier clothes. All friends, I noticed, were smoking. Inside I signed the book and looked at the picture boards. My gosh, she'd been pretty. Even as a little kid, she had one of those magical smiles that makes you want to trust or love or confide or buy. By the time she was fourteen or fifteen, she knew about the smile; you could tell. She had high cheekbones, black, black hair and eyes, skin you wanted to touch with the tip of your finger. And she was the star of every single photograph from the earliest on. Her images were alive, energetic, almost bursting into three dimensions. No doubt in my mind that if she had been a troubled soul, it had been of the Dylan Thomas rather than the Sylvia Plath variety.

"Peter?" Someone had taken my elbow, and I realized when I turned it must be one of her sisters.

"Yes?"

"Oh, I thought you might be. I'm Maud, Lisa's sister."

"Yes, I know. How in the world . . . ?"

"You do? Sophie, this is Peter." And Sophie took my one hand in both of hers.

"Oh, Peter."

"Wait a minute," I said.

"Tanya, this is Peter Carey," she said

"No, no," I said, but Tanya, who was nineteen or twenty, had already given me a quick, shy hug. "Peter *Ferry*," I said.

"Ferry? I thought it was Carey."

"I thought it was Cleary," Tanya said. "I thought Lisa said 'Cleary.'" She shrugged.

"Oh, well," said Sophie.

Now you may wonder why I didn't stop them right there and clarify things. Two reasons. First, I didn't know who Peter Carey or Cleary was, or if he was at all. Second, had I told them who I wasn't, I would have had to tell them who I *was*, with all the last-person-to-see-her-alive stuff, scenes of the accident, mea culpas. I didn't want that. It was clear that they were just barely hanging together to begin with. Still, I tried.

"I need to explain something."

"You need to explain nothing." Maud took me by the hand and walked with me. "No one could ever blame you for breaking up with her, believe me; we all know how difficult she could be. But we could also all see how good you were for her."

"No, no."

"We *could* see that. And we're very happy you came. Mother, it's Peter."

"Oh." I was lost. It was too late. I smiled and nodded and begged off when they asked me to sit with the family, sat in the back row and sneaked off as soon as the service began. If the real Peter Carey or Cleary showed up, they'd figure out their mistake. If he didn't, no harm done. I badly wanted to be finished with Lisa Kim; I really did. I wanted to say good-bye, close the box, put it in the ground, and walk away, but it wasn't going to be that easy. I was beginning to realize that I shared with this utter stranger an intimacy more intense than sex or confession or even betrayal. I was beginning to feel that it was more intense than any I'd known before.

John Thompson, the chair of my department, was looking through the window of my classroom door. He beckoned to me. "Just a minute," I said to the kids and stepped out into the hall.

"Sorry," he said. "I'm sorry, but there's a detective in my office to see you."

"A detective? Oh, the accident."

"Go take care of it. I'll sit in for you."

Lieutenant Carl Grassi was sitting at John's desk talking on his phone as if the place belonged to him, and he motioned me to sit down. He asked me to tell him about the accident. "I'm sure it's in the officer's report," I said.

"Just one more time," he said. I watched him as I talked. He was a bored, slightly hostile man who made no attempt whatsoever at civility. He affected a smirk as if it might have made him seem intelligent or worldly. "Couple more things," he said when I finished. "Where were you that day from noon until the time of the crash?"

"Me? Where was I? Well, I was here."

"Anyone see you?"

"Well, I taught until 3:15. My students saw me. Why are you asking me this?"

"Just answer the questions, okay? How about after that?"

He wanted to know if anyone had seen me after school and if I'd made any stops on the way home. When I said I'd bought a bottle of wine at Sunset Foods, he wanted to know if I had a receipt. I dug around in my wallet until I found it. The time on it was 6:17 P.M. Grassi took it with him.

On my lunch hour, I called Officer Lotts. "Sounds like they've got an open investigation of some kind," he said.

"Do you mean they suspect me of something?"

"Probably not. Probably just talking to everyone who saw her last. Process of elimination. Or maybe because you went to the funeral. If there's foul play, they watch the funerals."

"What kind of foul play?"

"I have no idea."

"Jesus," I said. "This bothers me; this scares me."

"Forget it," he said. "You're covered. If you hear from him again, call me; I'll find out what I can, but you don't have anything to worry about."

In the first Lisa Kim dream I had, we were sitting in the garden at La Choza. It was late October, but the sun was warm on our backs, bright on our faces. It was too high in the sky for the time of the evening; we wore big sweaters. We were all lovely. The women had white teeth and wisps of hair across their faces. We laughed and laughed. The air was golden. We were all friends, although I hadn't seen some of these people in years, didn't know a couple very well, didn't know one at all. Still, I felt closer to them, more comfortable with them than with my real friends, with myself. Perhaps we were stoned. Things moved slowly. Things tasted wonderful.

We were passing big platters of kamoosh: fried tortilla chips spread with beans, then melted yellow cheese, then guacamole. We were eating Steak Oaxaca: flour tortillas covered with chunks of carne asada, onions and cilantro, then melted white cheese. We were drinking beer from cans so icy they were hard to hold. We were holding them high in the air.

Someone toasted Carlos Zambrano, who had just pitched a no-hit, no-run perfect game striking out all twenty-seven Red Sox he had faced to win the World Series. I think we'd just come from Wrigley Field. It must have been a Sunday.

We toasted Ernie Banks for hitting a home run onto a rooftop across Waveland Avenue.

We toasted Bill Madlock for going four for four on the last day of the season to win the batting title.

We toasted Rick Reuschel for being so fat and graceful.

We toasted John Kenneth Galbraith for being so tall and old.

We toasted Dag Hammarskjold for giving his life for world peace.

We toasted Homer Simpson and Julia Child and Dave Van Ronk and Susan Sontag and Snoop Doggy Dogg. Then Lisa Kim appeared at the other end of the picnic table like a happy Banquo. She raised a champagne flute. She smiled that smile, her eyes locked on mine, and she shook her head a little bit as if to say, "I can't believe it." What she actually said was, "Here's to you, mister, and we both know for what."

On Saturday morning I bought a clothbound artist's sketch-book at Good's Art Supplies and took it down the street to Café Express, a coffeehouse full of secondhand couches and kitchen tables near our apartment in Evanston. I got a big ceramic mug of coffee and started writing. It was the first time in a long time that I'd written much of anything that wasn't of some utilitarian or commercial value, and I didn't quite know how to begin. I decided to make a list, a catalog I guess, of something that had been on my mind a lot: my near occasions of death. The first time I know I might have died was when I was two or three and I had a temperature of 104. My parents put me in a bathtub of cold water and ice cubes, and I screamed bloody murder. The first such event I remember was three or four years later, when I slipped off a jetty in Lake Michigan into a riptide and someone—I don't know who—just caught me by the back of my T-shirt. Then there was the cold spring weekend my family went to our summer home before the water was turned on or the phone activated. We built a huge banked fire in the living room and slept on mattresses around it. It turned out that the firebrick in the fireplace was old and bad and the heat had caused a smoldering fire in the wall behind. We all woke together in the middle of the night to a room filled with smoke. My brother and I rolled down our hill in pitch black to seek help while my parents kept the fire at bay with water, soda, milk, and then sand until the volunteer firefighters from Covert five miles away arrived.

Another time my dad got a headache working in the basement on a Sunday afternoon in January. He suspected a gas leak, but the two guys from the gas company found a carbon-monoxide leak instead and shut our furnace down. They said that we were lucky we didn't wait until Monday morning to call. I remember my dad forked over a good chunk of his life savings without a word of complaint to have the furnace replaced that very night, which turned out to be the coldest of the year. We lay in our beds beneath mounds of blankets and comforters listening to the workmen clanking in the basement beneath us. It was 3:00 A.M. when they fired up the new furnace, and the temperature in the house was 38 degrees. For a long time after that, I dated things from that day; the day we didn't die.

In my teens and twenties, I had several close calls that involved automobiles or alcohol—or both. Once my brother was trying to get my dad's Chevy station wagon up to 100 mph on a long, straight county road in rural Michigan. There was one blind spot on the whole stretch, and when we came over the rise, a 2½–ton farm truck was pulled across the road. The driver saw us and started forward, we braked hard and steered behind him, skidding right beneath his tailgate, which was cocked at a 45-degree angle and which scraped the hell out of the roof of the car.

Another time after playing softball and drinking beer, I was driving someone else's car way too fast on an unfamiliar road when I almost missed the same kind of curve Lisa Kim missed. I braked and slid sideways through the gravel and off the road into high grass. Had there been a ditch there, I would have rolled into it; and had there been a tree, I would have hit it very hard. Once, after helping friends move on a hot day, we were drinking beer and eating pizza on the roof of their new apartment building when we dared each other to walk the ledge around the perimeter. I still don't know how we all made it.

There were two airplane flights, one out of Columbus that hit a front like a stone wall on its initial ascent, and one into Quito, Ecuador, on a foggy night surrounded by the Andes when the pilot came in to land three times and roared off three times before he finally touched down the fourth time, and the flight attendants led the applause for what one of them said was "a very, very difficult landing."

Then there was a bump that turned out to be a sebaceous cyst, a heart murmur that disappeared, a lab test that was in error, and a bandit wearing a Yankees cap and a blue bandana over his face and holding a very small gun in his right hand who stepped out from the bushes when I was riding horseback in the hills of Jalisco in Mexico. He had me dismount, pull my wallet out and lie facedown in the dusty road. As he leaned to remove the Mexican currency from the wallet (he left the

American money), he put the gun against the back of my head. And those are only the close encounters I'm aware of. Who knows how many others I might have walked through or past like Mr. Magoo, with things crashing all around me.

When I finally put my pen down, it was afternoon, and I was exhausted. I had not expected to write so much or for so long; incidents came back one after another. I did not know how lucky I had been, nor how lucky any of us has to be to stay alive on this planet for very long. I closed my journal and went home.

The next day I made a second entry. This time I started writing down everything I could remember about Lisa Kim's accident. I guess, in a way, it was the beginning of this piece you are reading now.

In college I would hurry across the campus just to look in my mailbox, and the sight of one trim envelope through the little window would make my heart skip a beat. Now if I'm busy, I often don't open my box for two or three days at a time— nothing but bills, catalogs, and credit-card come-ons usually, seldom the kind of hand-addressed linen envelope I found there on a day late in January. The return address stopped me: Maud Kim Nho, Meadow Lane, Glenview. I stood right there in the vestibule and opened it.

First there was a note on stationery that matched the envelope written in a small, precise hand and green ink:

Dear Peter,
     I am taking the liberty of writing you after
considerable thought and at the risk of reopening

wounds that are now, I hope, beginning to heal. I
found this letter folded in the back of a book on Lisa's
nightstand. I have been looking at it and reading it
over for a couple weeks now. I've almost destroyed it
several times, both because of its intimate nature and
because Lisa had not sent it, and I can't be sure that
she intended to, but I can't bring myself to do so. It
is so full of her, of her energy and wit and intensity,
and we have so little of her left. At the same time, it is
not mine, and I feel like an eavesdropper reading it.
It is yours, and so I found your address in the guest
registry from the funeral and am sending it to you
to do with as you wish. I hope you don't mind.

Yours, Maud Kim Nho

Then there was a letter in bigger, bolder, black handwrit-
ing on typing paper:

P,

It is just dawn and I am just awake and you are on
my mind. Isn't that an old song? Funny how we always
talk in lyrics, you and I: all you need is love, what's
love got to do with it, many a tear has to fall. I love that
about you, your layers upon layers, your allusions, your
asides. A conversation with you needs footnotes and
a reader's guide. But then I love so much about you.
I am quite madly in love with you if you don't mind
my choice of words; see, now you have me doing it.

And why shouldn't we talk in lyrics? We are so
musical, my love. We are all about music, rhythm, beat,
and syncopation. We are a song, you and I. The first
time we did our dance moving together in the dark, it

wasn't sex, it wasn't fucking. It was breathing together, it was swaying, it was the two of us becoming a third thing for a moment, moments. I don't remember what happened to my clothes. I don't remember you touching me with your hands, not in the usual places, just my hair and upper arms and lightly on my hips. And then I realized you were inside me, but it was hardly the point, it was almost incidental, it was the way I always thought it should be (another song?). You can say that our little friend helped, but I don't think very much; what happened was inevitable.

That is how I feel about us, my darling. We are inevitable. We are inexorable. We are a juggernaut. I am very sad that we can not see each over Thanksgiving, but we shall, as always, have Tuesday, and then while we are apart, you will have this surprise missive to remind you of me. Besides, this thing we have is so strong that I don't need to see you. I am fine. I am happy, safe and secure in the warmth of our love though we are far apart and long away from each other. I love you deeply and eternally.

L

"Shit," I thought standing there, my hand unsteady by the time I had finished reading, looking about for fear someone would come along and catch me. "What do I do with this damn thing?" I thought. "Why did I have to read this?" I thought. "Why couldn't someone feel this way about me?" I thought. For the first time in almost three years, I badly wanted a cigarette.

3.

• • •

TRAVEL WRITING

DATELINE: CUERNAVACA, MEXICO
by Pete Ferry

On the ninth day of their march, (Cortes and his) troops arrived before the strong city of ... Cuernavaca. It was ... the most considerable place for wealth and population in this part of the country ... For, though the place stood at an elevation of between five and six thousand feet, it had a southern exposure so sheltered by the mountain barrier on the north that its climate was ... soft and genial.

—W. H. Prescott, *The Conquest of Mexico*

HERNANDO CORTÉS, Helen Hayes, and I were attracted to Cuernavaca by the same Chamber of Commerce sales pitch; the place has a damn near perfect climate. We all first went there on R and R. Señor Cortés was taking a break during his conquest of the Aztec Empire. Miss Hayes had just been crowned queen of the New York stage. And I was trying to get away from America for a while so I could look back at it and write about it. Truth be known, I badly wanted to be an expatriate. I guess I thought it would look good on my curriculum vitae. I was at that stage in my life where I defined myself by the things I did and the people I hung out with and, having recently found myself predictable and my life prosaic, my self-improvement plan was simple: Go somewhere interesting and hang out with better people.

And Cuernavaca is somewhere interesting. It sits just sixty-four miles south of Mexico City on the initial Pacific slope of the massive range of volcanoes that cluster around the capital. Beyond it to the south stretches the vast, verdant valley of Morelos that supplies many of the flowers we in the North pay so dearly for during the winter. Cuernavaca is all about flowers, cloudless winter skies, sidewalk cafés, swimming pools, and palm trees. Its mean winter and summer temperatures vary only two or three degrees either side of seventy-two.

It should not surprise you, then, that in addition to Cortés, Hayes, and myself, Cuernavaca has at one time or another attracted the likes of John Steinbeck, Merle Oberon, Ivan Illich, Anthony Quinn, Henry Kissinger, Erich Fromm, Gabriel García Márquez, the last shah of Iran, John Huston, and Malcolm Lowry, who set his novel *Under the Volcano* there, plus every Mexican luminary you can think of. These are the kind of people I went to Cuernavaca looking for, the kind I wanted to be with and be—artists and writers and freethinkers—but I found Charlie Duke instead. He introduced me to, among other things, the time-honored Cuernavaca pastime of name dropping and taught me the finer points of expatriation. In no time I fancied myself one of Steve Goodman's exiles from the old song "Banana Republics," hoping "to cure the spirit that's ailing from living in the land of the free."

Two roads leave the smoggy Valley of Mexico and cross the mountains to Cuernavaca. Both begin at an elevation of 7,400 feet, climb to 10,000 feet, and descend to 5,000, all in that sixty-four miles. And while travelers on one road can often see the other, the two take very different trips. It sometimes seems to me that the first is the road of the future. It is very handsome with bold red shoulders and flowering hedges dividing its four lanes. It is also an engineering marvel that sweeps in giant parabolas higher and higher to the very crest of the pass, where one can encounter snow in the winter and from which one can see what seems like the rest of the continent and, with a little imagination, the blue line of the Pacific Ocean on the horizon.

The second road belongs to the past. It corkscrews up the mountainside twisting and grunting every inch of the way. It goes through villages rather than past them, and beside it Indian women squat selling birds or beads or the tough Indian corn called *elote* which is boiled, slathered with mayonnaise and sprinkled with Parmesan cheese. This road travels across highland meadows, near alpine lakes and through forests of pine and spruce that defy every stereotype of Mexico, and at one point it passes a line of simple white crosses that mark the spot where, nearly eighty years ago, Francisco Serrano and other revolutionary leaders being transported to the capital as prisoners were lined up and gunned down by their guards.

The crosses always remind me that Maximilian and Carlota, their coach drawn by twelve white mules, used this ancient trail, and Benito Juárez in his black carriage and Stephen A. Austin, and perhaps even Cortés, or Montezuma, borne on his litter by six strong warriors.

Both roads are worth traveling. I suggest that you drive one down and the other back. Of course, you may intend to never come back, in which case you should take the old road.

And you should be informed that paradise appeals to everyone, even Mexicans, even the 99 percent of Mexicans who don't live in rococo mansions and go to the dentist in Houston. There are places in Cuernavaca set aside for cabdrivers and shopkeepers, and Los Canarios is one of them. This ramshackle resort was all Lydia Greene and I could find or afford the holiday weekend we first hit town.

Actually, Los Canarios sounded pretty good on paper: pool, garden, games, outdoor restaurant and bar, shops, palm trees, and lush vegetation. The problem was that all of this was shoehorned onto one small, seedy city block and most of it was dirty, dilapidated, and broken. Out on the street towering above the place was a big, broken sign dating, I suppose, from a time when the owners thought they might be able to attract wealthy Americans as guests. It read: LOS CANARIOS. HOTEL OF LUX.

Just across the street from Los Canarios is the other Cuernavaca. Las Mañanitas, an old hacienda that the city has grown out to surround, is one of the continent's loveliest small inns and restaurants. Behind its high walls topped with shards of broken glass one finds peacocks sitting on velvet lawns, cool blue pools, and perfect gardens. On the grass and verandas are a few quiet tables and many attendants in white jackets who pour your wine, light your cigarette and, on cool evenings, build fires in portable braziers just to warm your feet.

The last time I saw Charlie Duke, we ate dinner at Las Mañanitas. The first time I saw Charlie Duke, I was playing Frisbee with our dog Art out underneath the trees at Villa Katrina. Charlie came down the curving, cobblestone drive-way carrying a trayload of margaritas and hors d'oeuvres above his head.

The Villa Katrina was the weekend retreat of the German-Mexican Kronberg-Mueller family. It was situated on four acres of semiformal gardens that sloped down to a rugged barranco, or canyon stream, and consisted of a gatehouse; a main house complete with servants' quarters, red tile roof, balconies, and a vast veranda; and a three-bedroom fur-nished guest house. Charlie lived in the gatehouse. We had just rented the guest house.

Charlie was a tall, broad-shouldered, narrow-hipped, strikingly handsome man of forty-five whose manner, de-pending on your mood, could be described as genteel, effete, or even effeminate. Sitting on the bench out in the middle of the lawn, he talked an absolute blue streak, and he talked as if we were old friends, mentioning people, places, and events for whom and which I had no frame of reference. I went back to our bungalow that afternoon and laughed at him. What a boob. Almost at once Charlie became for me a sad emblem of what most expats really are: people who have way too much leisure time with which they do almost nothing but go out to lunch, drink, gossip, worry about their health, self-medicate, and complain about their gardeners.

But if Charlie was facile, he was also sincere. He insisted on adopting us and from that day on we became "the kids." He believed so strongly that we were friends that I didn't have the heart not to pretend we were, too.

Any doubt we had about Charlie's sexuality was dispelled by his constant talk of Stella. She was his "girlfriend" and lived in a hotel in town built around the ruins of the palace of Malintzin, Cortes's Indian mistress. Charlie said the hotel was lovely and the food among the best in Cuernavaca, so one night we went there to eat. Halfway through dinner the curtains were drawn on a private dining room across the veranda, and there sat Charlie, gaily drinking and playing cards with three women, the youngest of whom was at least seventy. Our food was only fair, and we left without saying hello.

For several weeks we felt like the lords of the Villa Katrina. The Kronberg-Muellers had yet to appear (we had rented through an agent), Charlie went on vacation, and the maid and gardener who lived behind the garage were seldom seen. We picked limes and bananas from the trees just outside our door, gamboled on the lawns, mused in the gardens, even sat on the grand veranda and dipped into the very Mexican pool. (Its elaborate imported pump and filter system had never been connected, and it could be filled only by garden hose, which took a couple of days by which time the water was already fairly dirty.) Then one morning I came home from my morning coffee downtown to find two gardeners at work, the windows all thrown open, rugs being beaten and linen aired. Shortly after that a chauffeur-driven Dodge Neon (it is one of the idiosyncrasies of Mexico that people are less expensive there than machines) rolled down the driveway and disgorged Mrs. Kronberg-Mueller herself, her town maid, her daughter Cynthia, and her sister Louise Speicher.

Katrina Kronberg-Mueller sat down on the veranda and stayed there. She was a stately lady of about eighty who kept a tiny silver bell at her side to ring for service. She spoke Spanish with an uncompromising Yankee accent that suggested that she found all those strange things native speakers did with their tongues and lips quite obscene.

Cynthia was in her forties. She wore too much makeup and her hair in a style that hadn't been popular since just after the Second World War. She belonged in an Edward Hopper painting. According to Charlie, Cynthia had had an unhappy marriage and a daughter who had taken up radical politics. So Cynthia had taken up poetry. She had published a slim volume with a San Francisco vanity press and talked of her editor as if he called her every other day.

One evening we were invited for drinks, and we entered the main house for the only time. We sipped sweet wine in the living room, which had the feel of a hunting lodge with its massive fireplace, and we listened to Katrina's life story.

Katrina met Señor Kronberg-Mueller at a party in Boston before the second war. He sang in a rich baritone, and she fell in love. After a whirlwind romance, they were married.

They sailed on a steamer for Veracruz and from there took the old narrow-gauge British-built rail line up and across the mountains to the capital.

Shortly after World War II, Señor Kronberg-Mueller built Villa Katrina as a present to his wife. Then he died. Katrina stayed in Mexico. Perhaps it was because she had a family there or two lovely homes, but I suspect it was because she had a place. She was an aristocrat. Had she been one in Boston before the war, she would not be one now. There was no aristocracy to go home to. In Mexico she could still ring her little silver bell.

And so, in a sense, could Lydia and I. We found ourselves admitted to some places and invited to others just because we were Americans, had fair skin, and spoke English. Actually, we were a couple of struggling artists, but no cold-water flat for us. We had a lovely house completely and tastefully furnished, French doors, red tile floors and gardens and gardeners outside every arching window all for a fraction of what it would have cost at home. Famous people were said to live next door and across the street. We were among—if not of—the elite.

So was Charlie Duke. He grew up in a small town in Kansas and married his first girlfriend while he was still a teenager. They had three kids in quick succession, and fought almost constantly. When the marriage broke, Charlie severed all ties and headed for Florida. There he attended college, taught, and worked at various sales jobs for several years. But the grass grew under his feet, and he began to explore the Caribbean on his vacations. One of his trips took him to Veracruz and then Mexico City, and he fell in love. He took a job teaching at an American school and settled in for the duration.

Before long Charlie met his second wife. She was somewhat older than he was and worked for Mexico City's English-language newspaper. As a result, she was on everyone's guest list. This was right up Charlie's alley. A natural gossip, he was born with a doily on his lap and a petit four between his finger and thumb.

"Sylvia got absolutely blotto, of course," he said. "We were mortified. She went on and on about poor Renaldo revealing the most intimate, the most scandalous . . . and, oh yes, we finally got the lowdown on the phony count. He has vanished, disappeared into thin air, and with one million pesos worth of Marta's negotiable bonds. Can you believe it? Not a trace. She has had a total breakdown and is in a sanitarium in Valle de Bravo."

"Uh-huh," I said. I did not know—nor had I ever heard of—a single one of these people, and I came to realize that Charlie's "we" included him and anyone else he knew, had been with or had seen. But if that anyone was you, his pretentiousness seemed harmless and was even sometimes flattering.

Charlie and his second wife lived in a luxurious villa in the San Angel colony of the capital and in their brief and glorious life together, they hit every embassy party, celebrity event, and costume ball in town.

"What happened?" I asked.

"We found out that the only thing we really had in common was drinking."

And so Charlie sought refuge in Cuernavaca, at first on

weekends at Las Mañanitas, and then more permanently at Villa Katrina. He sat on the porch of his tiny cottage, drank, and waited for people like us to happen by. He seemed to know everyone and to see no one.

All that changed in September when Charlie went back to school. Thereafter we saw little of him. Once he described his daily routine to me. He was up at 5:00 A.M. He showered, shaved, ate, listened to the radio, read, graded papers. He left for school at 6:30, stopping along the way to pick up riders: another teacher, two nurses and a young architectural student. After work he ran errands and shopped in the city, picked up the same crew for the return trip, and was home by 5:00. Between 5:00 and 7:00 he ate dinner, read, and drank a fifth of vodka. Then he went to bed.

"I am not an alcoholic," Charlie said. "I am a drunk."

"What's the difference?"

"There *is* a difference. An alcoholic *has* to drink. A drunk just *wants* to drink. I enjoy drinking. It's my hobby."

One night that fall Stella died. Charlie had never even mentioned that she was ill. "Oh, yes. Has been for years. Cirrhosis. She was an alcoholic," he said matter-of-factly.

Another night, Cynthia Kronberg-Mueller rapped on our door. It seemed that she had sent her chauffeur back to Mexico City and now, suddenly, unexpectedly, the maid had gone into labor. "Could you possibly ... would you mind terribly ..."

"No, no, of course not."

All the way down the hill into town, Cynthia crouched on our tiny backseat, talking. "And to think, this poor girl, barely more than a child herself ... *quantos años tiene?*"

"*Vientiuno.*"

"Just twenty-one. Twenty-one years old and a mother for the . . . *quantos niños tiene*?"

"*Cinco.*"

". . . for the sixth time. Can you imagine? It is so tragic. And look at her. Fat and worn out. Only a child herself. Sometimes I weep, Mr. Ferry, sometimes I weep for these poor, poor people." She stroked Elena's hair. "Poor, poor girl. *Pobrecita.*"

I prayed that Elena understood none of this. She sat beside me like a smug Buddha, hands clasped atop her latest blessed event. In truth, I don't think she cared very much for any of us. Hers was the slow, quiet revenge of the centuries. She did little work except during the odd weekend when the Kronberg-Muellers came down and, Charlie claimed, sometimes entertained her family and friends in the main house.

We moved into Mexico City before Elena and the baby came home from the clinic. It was there that Lydia had found a community of artists, studio space, and a gallery that was interested in showing her work. And while the quiet of Cuernavaca suited my needs as a writer, she had grown weary of its silliness and decadence and found herself longing for the hustle and hassle of a real city. Still, we came back often and, both ironically and predictably, it was only as visitors that we really got to know Cuernavaca and Charlie Duke as well.

One early Saturday morning we headed over the mountain and stopped first at Villa Katrina to let Art run free for half an hour. Charlie got up from his seat on the porch of his cottage as we walked down the drive. It wasn't noon yet, but he was stumbling drunk. He was embarrassing and embarrassed, and we went away quickly.

Later over lunch Lydia said, "You know, we invaded his privacy. That wasn't fair of us. We have to find a way to make that right." We decided to come again, this time announced, to invite Charlie to dinner and, I guess, to give him a chance to redeem himself. He did so with both the dignity and aplomb that only he can muster.

It was a cool night in January. We wore heavy sweaters and ate fresh red snapper in a restaurant garden. Charlie drank only beer and was full of stories about a new friend named Father Dick, a Trappist monk from County Kildare in Ireland who lived in a little monastery outside of town, said the English-language mass in the cathedral and had bought a ranch. He was going to make it the center of an agricultural co-op, and Charlie was going to build a house on it. I don't think we believed any of this, but we had a wonderful evening together and after Lydia had gone back to the hotel, Charlie and I finished up with a schooner or two at the open-air Café Universal on the plaza. I think that's when I heard about Charlie's past. And I remember that he asked me then about the writing I was doing and told me that he wanted to write, too, that he had a great story to tell about Cuernavaca.

"What is it?" I asked.

"No," he said wagging a finger and smiling. "You might steal it." I remember that because it was the only time I ever saw Charlie show any caution or distrust.

On another visit to Cuernavaca I met Father Dick. The three of us had dinner. Father Dick was a brawny, crew-cut, very shy man of about fifty. He spoke with a lisp and the reticence of someone who had spent many years in virtual silence. That evening ended early, however, because Charlie got sick. He was not taking his blood-pressure medicine, and he nearly fainted. I watched Father Dick drive away. Charlie sat beside him, his head lolling back over the seat.

The next time I saw Charlie, it was to say good-bye. A year had passed, our money had run out, and we had been unable to get the working papers that would allow us to stay. We drove over the mountain one final time, and as we walked around the grounds of Villa Katrina with Charlie, we were surprised to find the Kronberg-Muellers on their veranda. They invited us to lunch. We hadn't seen them since moving into Mexico City and took some time to get caught up. Then, after the usual discussion of Bolsheviks and gardeners, I said to Cynthia, "How's our baby?" I drew a blank stare.

"Elena's baby?"

"Oh yes, indeed," she recovered, "fine, fine, very good. Yes."

"Healthy and happy, I trust?" I asked.

"Oh quite healthy and happy. Yes, yes," Cynthia said.

"Is it a boy or a girl?" asked Lydia. Neither Katrina nor her sister Louise feigned knowledge, interest, or embarrassment, but Cynthia looked at me for a very long moment with a stupid smile on her face before Elena appeared and rescued her. "How is the baby?" I asked her. "A boy or a girl?"

"A little girl," she said.

"What do you call her?" Lydia asked.

"*Gordita*," she laughed, "the little fat one."

"May we see her?" I asked.

Elena brought the baby out in a big two-handled basket,

and we played with and held her as she giggled and kicked. She was nine months old.

During the next few years, Charlie proved to be a faithful if amusing correspondent. I knew just when he began each letter (when the bottle was full) and just when he finished it (when the bottle was empty). Each moved from coherence and even wit to non sequitur and confusion. There was the usual quota of people and events we had never heard of, but there was real information, too. Charlie's house on the ranch now had four walls and a roof, and he had moved in. In the meantime, his long-lost children had made contact, had come to visit and one—his eldest daughter—to live for a while.

We had news as well. We were back in Chicago with new careers and a new apartment in Evanston. Lydia was designing books for a publishing house and I was teaching. A year later, we flew to Mexico for a two-week winter vacation. We didn't tell Charlie we were coming because, frankly, we weren't sure we wanted to see him. After a few days in Mexico, however, we admitted to each other a bit sheepishly that we both did. There was something about Charlie Duke that drew us to him. I hoped without saying it that it was something more than being smugly amused by him.

Since Charlie had no telephone and only a P.O. box for an address, we went to his school in Mexico City. We stood for several minutes outside his classroom door watching as he worked at his desk with a gaggle of kids. He was a real teacher. Despite ample evidence, I'm not sure I had ever really believed this any more than I had believed anything Charlie told me. It was not that I thought Charlie a liar; it was just that virtually everything he said had the sound of bad fiction. He had a way of always choosing the least probable, most dramatic detail, and then embellishing it. "Father Dick didn't say a single word for twenty years. When he finally tried to speak, his voice wouldn't work for two weeks. Isn't that right, Father Dick?"

"Well, not quite."

Charlie's little house was also real. In fact, it was quite wonderful. It perched high on the mountain slope facing east toward rugged rock formations and cliffs, and above them on clear days the snowy peaks of the volcanoes. It was all of his own design, including a vaulted roof, great windows across the front, and a handsome stone veranda that ran the length of the place. We sat there one evening drinking margaritas while Father Dick (he had built a house just a stone's throw down the hillside) described the route of Cortés's army as he had traced and then walked it himself following Bernal Díaz del Castillo's explicit directions up this ravine and around behind that hillock and finally up through that pass there and then down to the Aztec capital of Tenochtitlán.

Charlie insisted that we abandon our hotel and come stay with him on the ranch. For the next few days, he took us to corners of the state I had never seen before: hidden forests and markets and mountain villages. We watched wood-carvers and stood in cool, ancient churches and shared a lunch of hot enchiladas and cold beer beneath a bright yellow awning. We ate big bowls of stew and told stories about each other late into the night. (I hadn't realized there were so many to tell.) And we talked with Father Dick who came to sit on the veranda in the evenings and watch the sun set.

Sunsets in that place are dramatic to the point of being histrionic. The actual disappearance of the sun is the least of it. That happens behind you if you are sitting on Charlie's veranda, and you may turn to glance at it or simply know it's going on by the absence of the sun's rays on the back of your neck. The real show is high above you, where for a long time after the shadows and evening cool have descended on you, it's still bright daylight on the mountain peaks and gleaming snowfields, and below you where in the depths of the valley it is dark night and the village lights have long since twinkled on. Seeing day and night all at once may tempt you to feel momentarily immortal, if there is such a thing, and when taken with a bit of red wine, to wax philosophic. We did some of that. One evening looking down into the village as if from on high, Father Dick said that a la Senator Paul Douglas, he had set out as a young man to save the world, and now he would be quite content to save this small place or even part of it.

"I don't suppose you'll ever leave here?" Lydia asked.

"Oh, yes," he said to our surprise, "I'll leave one day. When my work is done here, I'll go back to my community in Ireland. The monastery is my home, the community my family."

"I'll never leave this place," said Charlie.

"What place?" asked Lydia. "This ranch? Cuernavaca? Mexico?"

"This ranch near Cuernavaca in Mexico." It was just a clever answer until the next afternoon. Coming back to the ranch we discovered that a long-awaited calf had arrived. It was standing in the field on shaky legs beside its groggy mother. Charlie threw open the car door, got out, and did something quite unexpected. He started to undress. "Here." He handed me first his shirt and then his pants. Then, muttering something about needing to separate the calf from its mother, he stooped and gathered the little cow still wet with blood and afterbirth into his long arms. He hurried across the rocky pasture wearing only underpants and work boots, and I stumbled after him looking at his broad, strong back and realizing a rather astonishing thing. This silly man whom I'd been making fun of all this time was in possession of something I hadn't even started looking for and hadn't known until that moment that I wanted or needed. He was a complex, original, troubled, many-dimensional, self-invented, flawed and foolish but complete man, and he couldn't care less if I was laughing at him. He'd probably known all along.

That night we sat on the lawn at Las Mañanitas drinking cold white wine and eating *camarónes al mojo de ajo,* butterflied shrimp sautéed in garlic butter. It was our last night in Cuernavaca. There was wood smoke, the scent of flowers, some distant music and one of Charlie's stories in the air, and as I watched him tell it, I smiled at myself. Charlie was the guy I'd come to Mexico to find in the first place and I'd never realized it.

I shook my head. What a boob.

4

. . .

THE LOVE NAZI

I was not sure what I was looking for, exactly. It certainly wasn't Lisa Kim. I knew that she was dead; that much I knew for sure. But it may have been her tracks, her trail, evidence of her, clues about the woman who had written the letter that became for a period of time my most important possession.

Maybe I was trying to get rid of the letter. I was. I wanted to give the letter to Peter Carey or Peter Cleary and put an end to the strange sense of responsibility that had come with it. Responsibility was a thing I'd spent much of my life avoiding. It's why I lived in an apartment, drove an old car, and worked at a job in which my principal responsibility was to myself and to large children most of whom I could browbeat. It's why I lived with a woman who didn't want to get married, and with whom I had no children.

For a long time I thought of responsibility as the other side of freedom, and it was freedom that I most wanted. Not the ramblin'-man freedom of a thousand bad folk songs, although I'd listened to all of these and sung along with a few, but the freedom to live my life on my own terms. It's another reason—maybe the primary reason—that I love to travel; you're never freer than when your only responsibility is for yourself and a suitcase. My very personal definition of freedom dated to a time I'd hitchhiked to New Orleans in college. I was two days out of Chicago and somewhere south of St. Louis after I'd stayed up late the night before in Macomb, Illinois, when two soldiers picked me up. I fell asleep in their backseat in the warmth of the late-afternoon sun. When they turned off, they woke me and put me out on the highway, and I realized as I watched them pull away that I didn't even know what state I was in. I might have been in Missouri, I might have been in Arkansas, and since there had been some talk of Memphis, where I was headed that day, it was possible that we had crossed the river into Tennessee. I didn't know where I was, and neither did anyone else in the world except the two soldiers now gone. No one. I was frightened especially as the dusk came on, but the air was warm, the sky was clear, and there were fields beside the road in which I could have slept had I needed to, so almost at once my fear turned to something else. I knew in an instant that I'd never been so free, and might never be so free again. I was untethered from all I'd ever known, and when a car slowed to pick me up, I was a little disappointed.

Somehow over time I'd forgotten that feeling, but it had come back to me during the two weeks I'd spent alone in

Thailand over Christmas. Again I'd been frightened at first. I was tired to begin with and a bit spooked because we'd come in at night over Vietnam, and the Canadian helicopter pilot sitting beside me on the plane had pointed out the lights of Hue and the black winding ribbon of the Mekong River. Then I'd stepped onto the tarmac at midnight for fourteen days all by myself on the wrong side of the world with nothing but a *Lonely Planet* guidebook and the address of a cheap hotel I'd found in it. What if my appendix burst, I got run over, or the drunken shrimp fishermen I'd see a few days later in Hua Hin fighting with knives at dawn turned on me? But that, of course, is a part of freedom, and within a day or two, I began to feel comfortable with it and within a day or two more, to appreciate it.

You don't realize how often you tell lies until you aren't around the people you know. Not big lies, necessarily or usually. Little lies, but lots of them. Lies about where you want to go to dinner, or when you want to go to bed, or if you want one more glass of wine. How often you say you don't when you do, you can't when you can, you won't when you will. After a while, I began to think about big lies, too.

My only companions were E. M. Forster, a Dutch woman who helped me fix my camera, and an assortment of fellow travelers I fell in with, sat down beside or picked up at various stops along the way. I explored much of Bangkok on foot and much of Thonburi across the Chao Phya River by boat, slept in a berth on the night train to Chiang Mai, shared a communal room in a guesthouse there and played Ping-Pong on the lawn with some Swedish teenagers.

When I got home from Thailand, the apartment seemed

smaller and hotter. I almost immediately started lying again and resenting the people I lied to. And I lied to myself. For a month I told myself I was free of Lisa Kim. And then, suddenly, I was responsible for doing something about this damned letter, and after all that freedom, there was a small part of me that liked it, that felt somehow liberated from irresponsibility and surprisingly relieved to be so. And so there I was pulled in two very different directions by a feeling so old I'd nearly forgotten it, and another so new I'd never experienced it; by a desire for freedom and a need to finally be responsible for something in my life. And why all of this was suddenly happening to me I did not know, except that I was pretty sure it wouldn't be happening if it were not for Lisa Kim, so I went looking for her.

I could not find Peter Carey or Peter Cleary in the phone book, nor Peter Kerry, nor Peter Carray. All the Careys, Clearys, Kerrys, and Carrays I called said "wrong number" when I asked for Peter. The doctors Kim *were* in the book. Theirs was a large, comfortable, but not ostentatious white clapboard house on a leafy, brick side street a few blocks from Lake Michigan. Its only distinctive feature was a bright yellow front door that I thought instantly must have been Lisa's idea. Otherwise it was almost nondescript, and I wondered if the Kims, like so many Asian Americans I had known, simply wanted to slip into, fold into society. Down the alley there was a functional two-car garage and in the backyard, a modest flower garden that did not draw attention to itself.

New Trier High School looked like a high school does in the movies. The security guard at the front door sent me to the security office. There a man at a counter looked at my ID.

"I'm a freelancer writing for the *Tribune*. I'm doing research for an article on New Trier grads who are doing things in theater and movies and stuff like that." He issued me a pass, and I climbed to the third floor, where the library occupies a large corner of the building.

I asked for the yearbook for Lisa Kim's graduation year, the one for the previous year, and the one for the next year. I sat beside four girls who were chatting and doing homework at the same time. They kept looking at me as if they recognized me from somewhere. I suppose it was really because they *didn't* recognize me, because I was an anomalous adult. I certainly felt out of place. I also felt a mixture of guilt and resentment. The guilt was because I had begun to conceal things from Lydia; she did not know that I was here, for instance, trying to find out something about Lisa Kim. Had she known, she would have shaken her head and rolled her eyes; she was treating me like a little boy and acting as if Lisa Kim were the wounded bird or mangy dog I'd brought home. That's where the resentment came from. In truth, Lydia was not the only one. I'd been taking a good bit of shit and getting a good bit of gratuitous advice about the whole thing.

My gosh, Lisa Kim was a lovely girl.

LISA LOUISA KIM
"To try when there is little hope is to risk failure. Not to try at all is to guarantee it." Anonymous. The unKorean. The antiKorean. Fire. Love to Mother Rosalie and the C's. Thanks to Friedrich Nietzsche. Volleyball 1; SADD 1; Talent Show 2,3,4; *Bye Bye Birdie 2, Little Shop of Horrors* 3; *Hedda Gabler* 3; *Oklahoma!* 4; *Death of a Salesman* 4; Senior One-Acts 4.

I looked for Peter in all three books. Nothing. I read Lisa's entry over again. Then I began to slowly read other entries. I found Annie Pritchard, who was also in *Hedda Gabler, Oklahoma!*, and the Senior One-Acts. Her entry included the designation "Water." Fire; water. It took me a while to find Wind. She was Hannah "Sammy" Stone. She was not a theater kid, but she did thank Mama Rosalie and wrote, "Go C's!" I could not find Earth. I went through each entry twice.

I decided to look for Peter in the other books. No luck, but in the earlier one I came across Rosalie Belcher, a senior when Lisa had been a junior who had been in the cast of both *Bye Bye Birdie* and *Little Shop of Horrors*. In addition, she called herself "C Earth Mother."

I found Annie Pritchard in the Chicago phone book and called her. She thought I was a salesman. "No, no," I said. "Listen, don't hang up. It's about Lisa Kim."

"Lisa? What about Lisa?" I told her most of the story. I told her most of the truth.

"So who are you exactly?" I told her most of that, too. "I'm sorry, what exactly do you want?"

"There's a guy named Peter Carey or Peter Cleary that Lisa went with."

"I know Pete Carey. We worked together at John Barleycorn."

"John Barleycorn?"

"He's a bartender. I'm a waitress slash actor, just like Lisa."

"Anyway, I have a letter Lisa wrote this guy, and I just want to get it to him."

There was a long pause. "What kind of letter?"

"A personal one."

"Well," she said, "I guess you could send it to me. I guess I could get it to Peter."

"You think you could?"

"I think I could. Let me give you my address. I'll get it to him."

"Okay, yeah," I said, "that would be good. Or you could tell me where to find him and I could do it."

"I think maybe I should do it. He knows me. He was pretty broken up." She paused. "Lisa was sort of the love of his life."

"Okay. Sure."

I never sent it to her. I guess I didn't want her to see what Lisa had written, to pass it around like a bag of chips. I mean, I wasn't even sure they were friends at the end. Or maybe it was because I wanted to see Peter Carey myself.

I talked to a bartender, an assistant manager, and the manager at John Barleycorn. The manager said, "Sure, I remember Pete. Fact, someone just called me looking for a reference for him. Let's see. I think it was Paddy Shea's."

Paddy Shea's even smelled like an Irish pub. They must have brought the whole thing over. I sat at the end of the bar nursing a Guinness, reading the *Sun-Times* and watching Peter Carey move back and forth behind the bar. It was slow in the midafternoon, and he was washing glasses and restocking. He did not notice me watching, and I liked that about him. Still, he was not what I expected. He had an easy smile, an easy manner, and those sloe eyes romance novelists say that women like, but he was pigeon-toed, a bit soft in the middle, and his dark, wavy hair started up high on his forehead.

When he brought me a second pint, I said, "You're Pete Carey, aren't you?"

"Right," he said.

"I met you once someplace. I'm a friend of Lisa Kim's."

"No shit. Man, too bad about ol' Lisa." It wasn't the response I'd expected, but I went on.

"I guess you two were pretty close."

"Not really." He moved down the bar for a while.

When he came back, I said, "Listen, Pete, I have something that belongs to you."

"Me?"

I explained briefly and put the letter on the bar. He didn't even pick it up. He was drying a glass on his apron, and he read it quickly with a raised brow. "That can't be for me, pal."

"I think it is."

"None of that stuff means anything to me. You know, she and I . . . we hung out a couple times last summer, but she was too much work. Sorry if you're a friend or something. That was it. We didn't have a love affair. We did the old Jimmy Buffett a time or two; that was all." He moved down the bar again. I read the letter over, wondering if I could have misunderstood it. I finished my pint and left. I didn't say good-bye.

For a few weeks I did nothing. As winter softened slightly and turned grudgingly toward spring, I pretended to have put the whole thing behind me in the hopes that people would stop treating me like a dotty aunt. In truth I was waiting to know what I should do next. In the beginning I'd been passive; I hadn't done anything except go to the funeral. Everything else had come to me. Now I was becoming an active agent, if a cautious one. I folded Lisa's letter and kept it in my hip pocket with my wallet, but I did not forget it. I was bothered by the fact that Annie Pritchard had misrepresented Peter Carey's feelings for Lisa. Or he had. And I was bothered that she seemed reluctant to tell me how to find him. Why was that? And who the hell was the letter intended for, if not for Peter Carey? While I waited, I went about my life. I had classes to teach, papers to grade, tests to write. And then I had a relationship to work on. Lydia and I went out to dinner on Friday nights, shopped, cleaned and washed on Saturday, saw friends occasionally, took in a movie, watched TV, even tried to play Scrabble once or twice, but my heart wasn't really in any of it. In reality I was becoming the worst things you can be in a relationship: distracted and indifferent. Or maybe I'd always been these things and she had, too, but now she wasn't anymore.

One night I couldn't sleep, so I got out of bed, made myself a mug of tea, and sat in the shadows of our bedroom on the easy chair where we threw our clothes and looked at Lydia sleeping in the moonlight, her slightly Roman nose, her full lips, her wild tangle of red hair. It was the hair that I'd first noticed about her. Actually, it had been pointed out to me across a party. "See that hair," Tom MacMillan had said, "bet you her thatch is just like that." My, we were young and foolish, but even then—even at twenty-two—Lydia had had a bearing, had carried herself just so (it was in the roll of her hips, the cock of her head, the way she threw her shoulders back) as if to say, "I don't owe nobody nothing."

And she didn't, by the way. Lydia was the one person I knew at that age who had done virtually everything for herself if only by default, if only because her parents were such emotional cripples. When she was fourteen, Lydia started taking orders in a pizzeria and saving for college, even though when her father got wind of her plans, he told her, "Don't expect me to help." She didn't. Without her parents even knowing it, she applied to a good private high school and got a scholarship. All through high school she worked thirty hours a week as a waitress in an IHOP. She got a full ride to Bennington, and when her parents expressed an interest in attending her graduation (they had never even seen the school), she asked them not to. She didn't give them an explanation because she didn't owe them one. That's one of many things I learned from Lydia Greene. Never offer an excuse, even if you have a good one. When she called in sick, she never coughed or wheezed or made her voice sound weak or faint; she just said, "I'm taking a sick day and won't be in today." Back then Lydia was self-sufficient in every way I could see, and that's what really made her attractive to me; she was maintenance free. Now she wasn't anymore.

I got up and made myself another cup of tea. When I sat back down, Lydia had turned over and I could no longer see her face. I began to think about Lisa Kim, and I realized that I knew what to do next. In the morning I called her old high-school friend Annie Pritchard, who had wanted me to send her Lisa's letter. I apologized for not having done so. "Been so busy, and I thought maybe I could hand it to you. Maybe I could buy you a cup of coffee or a beer or something."

I did not show my photocopy of Annie Pritchard's graduation picture to her; she would not have liked it. If she had ever been that pretty, she wasn't anymore. If she hadn't, the photographer had done her no favors; she could only look at it and remember what had never been.

We met in a bar near Lincoln Square. She was sitting at a cocktail table, her long legs crossed beneath, sipping a glass of white wine that I would discover later she had not paid for. She was tall and emaciated. Her arms were uniformly thin and without definition; you could probably touch thumb to finger around both her wrist and bicep. I sat across from her as she read the letter carefully and slowly. Then she put it in her purse and said, "They were very much in love. They were going to move in together. Lisa even said that they had talked about getting married, although that would have been so unLisa. I will see that Peter gets this. I think he'll want it. Thank you."

"He doesn't want it," I said. She looked up. "I saw him. He wasn't in love with Lisa Kim. They had a brief fling a while ago. So I'm just curious; why are you making this up?"

"I didn't make it up," she said without embarrassment. "Lisa did. It was for her family. You know, they're so conservative. They wanted her to settle down, blah blah blah. She thought if she had a boyfriend, they might get off her back."

"It seems like kind of an elaborate lie. I mean, how do you explain the letter? Did she plant it to be found? And would she want her mother reading stuff like this?"

Annie Pritchard took the letter back out and read it again. Her eyebrows went up her forehead, and she began to smile slightly. She tossed it on the table between us. "Peter," she began slowly, "what do you really know about Lisa?"

"Very little, really."

She put her fingertips together and looked above my head. A waitress took our order, and Annie Pritchard waited until she was gone. "Lisa Kim was brilliant. Lisa Kim was trouble. She was brilliant trouble. She was the most natural actor I've ever seen. She created the role of Lucy Fantisima in *Gangbusters*. That's her masterpiece, and it's all hers. Everyone who has played it since her has done nothing, nothing but imitate Lisa, even Mandy Mejias. They're still imitating her on Broadway right now. Did you see the film? Same thing. Lisa should have had that part, but she was just too damn much trouble." Annie Pritchard had a way of watching you for your reaction before you had one. It struck me as adolescent. "Trouble was, she never stopped acting. It was all a performance, and you could never say 'scene.' She wouldn't stop. It drove you fucking nuts. She was the manic without the depressive. She was always on. She was like a drug; the first few minutes were exhilarating, but she got old fast."

"You know," I said, "I didn't know her, and I never will, but 'P' did, and he may have loved her, and I'd like to find out who he is and give him this letter. That's all. I just thought maybe you'd be able to help me . . ." I started to get up.

"Hang on," she said. "Listen, this stuff is not about love. It's not about Peter Carey. What it's about, it's about drugs . . ." She was watching me like that again.

"Drugs?"

"It's about heroin. It's all in code. 'Our little friend.' Get it? Thanksgiving is a euphemism for the rush you feel. That shit about music; when you're high it's like singing a song, holding a note."

"Are you telling me that Lisa Kim was a heroin addict?"

"Don't be so Katie Couric. The trick with heroin—the real thrill—is to control it and not be controlled by it. And people do. Katie doesn't want you to know that. People use it for years, decades, their whole lives."

I looked up at her. "Do you use it?"

"We all use it," she said, defining a group, as if to point out that I wasn't and would never be part of it.

"Well," I said, "it doesn't sound as if Lisa was very much in control of it."

"No," she said.

"You're amused. Wasn't Lisa your friend?"

"My friend? I knew her a long time. We spent time together. But if you mean were we blood sisters, did we pledge our fidelity—she caught the waitress's eye as she passed and ordered another glass of wine—did we promise to always be there for each other? I'll tell you what we promised. We promised to do whatever we could to feel the most alive. If that was being 'true' to each other, so be it. If it was being untrue, fucking each other, betraying the other person, okay, too. We don't believe in friendship in the cheesy, conventional meaning of the word," she said a little proudly. "Let me put it this way: Lisa and I were part of each other's experience. In that sense, we were part of each other."

"Then I suppose you don't believe in love, either?" She just stared at me. "And my trying to track down this 'P' is just silly. Or maybe he doesn't even exist."

"Oh, he exists, all right. He's a drug dealer. That's who 'P' is. That's who Peter Carey is."

———

Annie Pritchard disgusted me, drinking my wine while holding me in contempt like a teenager to a parent or that certain type of late-century wife who resented the hell out of her husband while maxing out his charge cards. Her story sounded as if she were making it up as she went along. She managed to order one more glass of wine before I paid for the drinks. Leaving the bar, I thought about dropping the whole thing, and I crumpled the letter and tossed it in a garbage can on the street, got in my car, drove around the block, and plucked it out again.

It wasn't going to be that easy. Besides, I didn't want to drop it. It had somehow become too important to me (I ignored the creeping fear that that was because nothing else was), but again I didn't know what to do next, so again I waited. Then one blustery Saturday morning a couple of weeks later, between the hardware store and the grocery store, I bought a paper and stopped at Café Express to read it and put something warm into myself. Other people had the same idea, and there were no empty tables. I was waiting for one to open when I saw Tanya Kim, and she saw me. Perhaps I was looking for her; we both lived in Evanston, only a few blocks apart, and Café Express was exactly the kind of place she'd hang out. At any rate, she had an extra chair, so she beckoned and I sat down. She seemed pleased to see me, as I was always pleased to run into my older brother's friends or girlfriends. And even though I was neither one of those things, I was happy to see her; we had a funny little bond, the two of us, that wasn't based on friendship or affection but rather on shared trauma, and it invited us to be confidential with each other, if shyly, even though we were strangers.

"How you doing?" I tried to sound as if she didn't have to answer if she didn't want to.

"Better," she said. "It gets easier." I studied her face; you would have picked them out as sisters anywhere. Tanya had all of Lisa's features, but they were put together a little differently. She wasn't nearly as pretty. Whatever the intangible thing is that defines beauty, she just didn't have it.

"And your parents?"

She said her father was permanently sad, but her mother was "being more Asian about it." When she asked about me, I had a chance to tell her the truth, but I didn't. "I'm okay," I said.

Then she asked unexpectedly, "You know what the worst part of it is? Now they're afraid of losing me. I have absolutely no freedom. For years they were too busy to even notice me; now they're all over my ass. And once a week I have to go up there and worship at the shrine of the sainted Lisa. I'm sorry. I'm sorry. You're catching me at a bad moment." She got up to go to work, pointing through the plate-glass window at a camping-and-hiking store called Outfitters across the street.

"I thought you were still in school," I said.

"I work weekends. Look, I shouldn't have said anything. It's just that they've turned her into something she wasn't. I'm sorry; I know you say you loved her, but to me she was a selfish bitch. She never remembered a birthday. She never called unless she wanted something. She was a bitch who slept around—I'm sorry—did drugs, a fact we have conveniently completely blocked out, and didn't give a shit about anyone but herself."

"Did Lisa do a lot of drugs?" I asked.

She cocked her head. "Why are you asking me? I rarely saw her. None of us saw her, really. If anyone should know, you should. Did she do drugs?"

"Not with me."

"Well, she did with someone. You really didn't do drugs with her? See, we were right about you. Honest to God, I think you could have saved her."

"Oh, don't say that." I could just imagine Lydia and Steve cringing. "No one can save anyone," I said, and if I believed that, I also believed that I was somehow involved in something that was inevitable. "And what do you mean, 'someone did'? Did you ever see her doing drugs? Do you know this for sure?"

"Yes," she said finally, firmly.

"If you didn't see her much, may I ask how you know?"

"No. I don't know. I gotta go." She stood up.

"Tanya, you're really leaving me hanging. I mean, it's not as if I asked. You kinda brought it up. Can't you tell me?"

"I don't know. What's your phone number?" She punched it into her phone.

It saddens me that with virtually everyone in this world looking for someone to love, so many of us can't find anyone, or find the wrong person, or find too many people. Love is so damn hard. Falling in love isn't. Falling in love is easy, but being in love is hard, and staying in love is harder.

Falling in love is easy and fun. I do it all the time and always have. As soon as I sit down on a plane or in a ball game or restaurant, I look for someone to fall in love with.

And every year I fall a little bit in love with one or two high school girls. Sometimes they are in my class, sometimes they are just kids in the hallway, but every day I look forward to seeing them. They are like lovely watercolors or wistful little tunes you can't get out of your head. Life is more interesting when you have a little crush on someone.

But being in love. Perhaps the only thing harder than being in love is not being in love. I saw somewhere the other day that a crab boat was missing in the far north Pacific, and I thought of Bobby Quinn. He was a terribly shy, terribly lonely boy I met in Thailand at Christmastime who worked on one of those boats and had come halfway around the world looking for a girl to take back to Unalaska Island with him, to take to sea with him. He had found her, too, he thought. Her name was Sahli, and she was as shy and desperate as he was. She would have to have been.

Sahli was a prostitute. I often wonder if she went back with him. For some reason, I picture her squatting on her haunches as Thai women do on the deck of a ship cooking something over a burner. The images are as incongruous as was their odd little love. I hope they weren't on that ship that was lost.

After seeing her sister, I had a second dream about Lisa Kim. This one was an erotic dream. Actually it was a wet dream. In it Lisa's hair ran through my fingers over and over like cool water. I touched her cheek with the back of my forefinger. It was as soft as a breeze. She was squirming toward me. Squirming and squirming. I couldn't get hold of her.

When I woke up, Lydia was lying on her side looking

right at me. She rolled onto her other side turning her back toward me. I started to touch her shoulder, but I didn't know what to do or what to say, so I didn't do or say anything.

"Why don't you want us to write stories about love?" asks the girl whose hair has turned purple.

"It is just that they are hard to write, that's all. Hemingway said to write about what you know; write about events, things happening, things you've seen happen. A fight. An argument."

"Are you saying that we don't know about love?" asks someone else.

"I'm saying love is an enormously complex thing. I'm not sure that anyone who is eighteen knows enough about it to write about it very well."

"I suppose *you* do?" says the purple-haired girl. "I mean, who in this room fell in love with a fictional dead woman? Raise your hand."

"I did not fall in love with Lisa Kim," I say, "but your point is well taken, and in a way it's what I'm saying. Love is a tough nut. You can write about lust. You can certainly write about infatuation."

"Aren't those aspects of love?" asks Nick.

"Sure."

"Why are you patronizing us?" he continues.

"Am I? I guess I am, so I'll stop. You can write about anything you want. Here's what I'm saying: Most successful pieces are about things the writer understands well, and love is hard to understand at any age, including eighteen, maybe especially eighteen. I know I knew little about it at that age. And

I don't mean to insult you, though I probably have, but most teenage stories about love just aren't very good, so I would gently steer you toward topics you are expert about: parents, families, friends, school, brothers and sisters, adult hypocrisy, the uses and misuses of power and authority, bad teachers. Kids often write great stories about topics like these. Kids less often write great stories about love. That's all I mean."

"What's so hard about love?" asks the dog-faced boy.

"Oh, please!" says a girl. "As if you know the slightest thing about it."

"Then tell me: What's so hard about it?"

"It hurts," says the girl.

"Always?"

"It can hurt," says the girl. "It has great potential to hurt. When you don't have it, all you can think about is getting it. When you get it, all you can think about is losing it."

"And when you lose it . . ." The girl with purple hair shakes her head. "My parents divorced when my brother and I were very young. I hardly remember them together. He remembers a little better. Neither one remarried; well, my dad did, but briefly. It didn't work. My mom never did. Now all these years later, they can barely talk to each other. They can barely stand to be in the same room." She goes on to tell us a quite amazing story. Recently her father had handed her a box of photographs he was about to throw out saying, offhandedly, that maybe she'd like them. She sat cross-legged on her bed and looked at every one, studied them. They were from the early years: her parents dating, her parents dancing and on vacation in Mexico with long hair and bell-bottoms, arms around each other, the wedding, feeding each other cake and of course they were photographs, so most of them are posed. But there was one in particular that wasn't: Her dad was telling a joke. He was standing up with a party hat on, arms spread and everyone in the picture was laughing, and no one harder than her mother who had tears in her eyes and one hand to her chest; she was so proud of him and in love with him, the purple-haired girl could see it in her face. "I couldn't stop looking at that picture," she says. "I'd never seen them in love. I never knew that they ever had been. But in that picture and some of the others, they clearly were. I kept that one and used it as a bookmark; I would take it out when I was in a boring class—never yours, Mr. Ferry—"

"Of course not."

"—and look at it, because I don't know why. I just would. I think it was important to me to discover that I was conceived in love, something I never knew, something I'd never even considered a possibility. Finally I framed that picture and put it by my bed." Then one day the purple-haired girl noticed that it was gone. She asked her mother what had happened to it. Her mother said she had thrown it away. The girl flipped out. She said what right did her mother have to touch her personal property? "She said it wasn't mine, it was hers. She said she didn't want me to look at it because it distorted the truth; it was a lie. I think *she* didn't want to look at it because it contained a truth, one it's too hard for her to face."

"Write that," I say.

"What?"

"There's your story. Write that."

"Yeah," says the dog-faced boy, "write it just like you told it."

"If you do, it will contain a truth, too," I say.

"What truth?" asks the purple-haired girl.

"You tell me."

"That love sucks," says someone.

"That love is a lot like hate."

"That love can turn into hate."

"Easily," I say.

"How about that love is not eternal. That love is fleeting," says Nick. "That for all our wishing it would, love doesn't last."

"How about we say, 'Love is not necessarily eternal'?" I say.

"Now you're equivocating," says Nick.

"Big word," says someone.

"From *Macbeth*," says Nick.

"I don't think—" I start.

"Sure you do," says Nick. "I mean, 'love is not necessarily eternal' is obvious, right? I mean, look at Hollywood; look at her parents. Duh. But 'love is not eternal' is news. 'Love is not eternal' is Truth with a capital T."

"I'm just not sure that it is true," I say.

"Oh, Mr. Ferry, you're a romantic," someone says.

"No—"

"Sure you are. You fell in love with the girl in the car, a character you made up, or say you made up, at least."

"Well—"

"Is that it?" asks Nick. "Are only the romantics allowed to write about love?"

"That's not at all what I meant," I say.

"Oh, Mr. Ferry," says the girl with purple hair, "you're a love Nazi. Yes you are; you're the Nazi of love."

5

• • •

TRAVEL WRITING

DATELINE: BANGKOK AND CHIANG MAI, THAILAND
by Pete Ferry

While neither Thai nor American officials like to talk about it, prostitution is a major industry in Thailand. It is in small part a legacy of the Vietnam War, during which Bangkok was an important center for American soldiers on R and R, but more a product of ancient cultural and very modern economic factors. Whatever its origins and explanations, prostitution in Thailand is a phenomenon that the visitor can neither ignore nor escape.

WHEN I CAME TO Thailand, I wasn't looking for a woman," said Bobby Quinn. "I had no intention of, ah, hiring a prostitute. And now look at me; I've got two of them." One was sitting next to him and across from me at the big table of Westerners, all of us eating and drinking. Her name was Sahli. She was a slender girl with feline features, light brown skin and long black hair. She seemed very shy, and neither of us thought that she spoke English. As we poured ourselves another beer, she quietly nursed a Green Spot orange soda.

The other one was back in Bangkok. "I gave her a vacation when I came here to Chiang Mai," said Bobby.

"How did you find the one in Bangkok?"

"Well, the first cab I got in, the driver asked if I wanted a woman. I said no, and he said, 'Why not take a look? No obligation. It doesn't cost anything to look.' So there I was in this massage parlor with maybe thirty, forty girls, and, you know, then I'm walking out with one, and I've bought her for two weeks."

"How much?"

"Thirty bucks a day, but I know I got taken. I could have had her for twenty. I got this one for twenty." He nodded toward Sahli. She got up quickly, left the table, and hurried out the door of the restaurant.

"My God, Bobby," I said. "I think she understood what we were saying."

"I don't think so."

"Maybe you should go after her?"

"She'll be all right."

"Would you mind if I went, then?" I asked him. I found her standing by the river with her back to me. I approached her, but not too close. I spoke softly. I decided to speak in English, just as if she understood. "Sahli, what we said was very thoughtless. We have hurt your feelings and we are very sorry. We all feel very bad." I stood beside her, but not too close. I talked about the beauty of the river, Chiang Mai, and northern Thailand. After a bit, I smiled at her and motioned with my hand: "Would you like to go back in?"

She hesitated, but came, her arms still crossed on her chest. We sat side by side at the table, and neither of us took part in the conversation.

Bobby Quinn made his living fishing for Alaska king crab. He shipped out of Unalaska Island in the Aleutians. His work was very lucrative, but very dangerous. He was twenty-eight years old and had been crabbing for seven years. The year before he had gone to sea just twice: once for thirty days, once for forty-two. On these two trips he had made enough to live well and travel around the world. Still, "Ships always go down, people always get washed over." He felt sometimes that he was living on borrowed time. His brother, who lured him to Alaska to begin with, wouldn't go out anymore. Bobby said simply, "I am looking for another line of work," but one sensed that it would be tough for him to give up the money and the freedom.

Bobby was tall, reed thin, and almost handsome. He had huge doe eyes and a hesitant, shy manner. When I knew him better, he admitted that he had, indeed, come to Thailand looking for a woman. He was not alone.

Bangkok is the brothel of Asia, and the typical tourist is a single male between the ages of twenty and fifty from Australia, Japan, Arab countries such as Kuwait and Saudi Arabia and European countries such as Germany. In fact it is so comparatively rare to see a single Western woman here that you almost blush when you do as if you have encountered your sister when you are leaving an adult bookstore. The whole city has a slightly sordid quality to it. There are peep shows, freak shows, and live sex shows. There is the famous Bangkok massage which can even include a massage and, of course, there is the conventional roll in the hay at every turn; every hotel permits prostitutes to ply their trade (even the most expensive and exclusive) and every cabdriver is a procurer. The buyer can contract for any sexual service at a fraction of what it would cost in Tokyo, Paris, or New York.

But it is more than economics and availability that give Thai prostitution its unique character. That comes from services Thai prostitutes are willing to provide that are not sexual. "They call them temporary wives," said Bobby. "They do your wash, bathe you, polish your shoes while you sleep, go out and get your food, take care of you if you are sick, laugh at your jokes, rub your back. It's wonderful." Thai prostitutes sell companionship and more. They sell the illusion of love—temporary love—and perhaps even love itself sometimes. It is always dangerous to put a good face on anything as insidious and evil as prostitution, but I could not deny my feeling that there was something human happening there. We all need so desperately to be loved.

I thought while in Thailand about an old friend who visited Bangkok some years ago. Now he is a prominent Chicago attorney, but then he was just a kid on a once-in-a-lifetime around-the-world jaunt. He told me later in hushed tones about a Thai girl who had fallen for him. Yes, she was a prostitute. Still—he would awaken to find her watching him. She loved to hear him talk, so he talked and talked. She cried when he left, so he gave her half his money. "She asked me to take her with me and I'll tell you"—he smiled a little sheepishly—"I actually thought about it for a minute."

When I first arrived in Bangkok after twenty-one hours on planes and in airports, I headed right for the hotel bar. It was 10:00 P.M. I ordered a Singha beer and made a few notes. A young Thai woman was sitting beside me smoking, talking quietly with the female bartender. She seemed bored, perhaps sad. Suddenly two big Australians burst in. They were all backslaps, wet kisses, and beer. Before I went to bed, one of them was folded around the Thai woman. He was saying hoarsely and not very discreetly, "Okay, okay, okay. I don't care what you was last night. Last night is gone forever. All I care about is tonight, and all I know is that tonight you are my lady."

At 7:00 the next morning, the coffee shop was full of young Arabs and their Thai girlfriends, who were working the early shift because their boyfriends don't drink. (The girlfriends of Australians didn't come on duty until somewhat later in the day.) They were all having Cokes and Marlboros for breakfast and beating time on the tabletops to loud rock-and-roll tunes. One couple drank from two separate straws but one glass; the atmosphere was sort of Third World malt shop. Then a Thai girlfriend huffed through the room, and her large African boyfriend hurried anxiously after her. They both looked as if he had just insulted her meaf loaf.

I read a guidebook, ate toast, drank canned orange juice. People who came into the room glanced at me a bit curiously. I felt conspicuously alone. It is a feeling I had throughout my visit to Thailand. "Is he a priest? A cop? A queer?" Occasionally I felt the need to explain, even somehow apologize. "I'm committed, you see . . . made a promise . . . professional objectivity . . ." I didn't mention my obsessive fear of AIDS because no one else seemed at all concerned. "Oh, a doctor checks the girls every week. They all carry condoms," an American I met said blithely. "They really got it under control here. Asian success story . . . you can read about it." Besides, it seemed a bit like talking about plane crashes at 30,000 feet.

On the bus going toward the center of Bangkok, I studied the hotel brochure because it had a map of the city. I noticed two pictures—one taken in the lobby, one in the coffee shop—of very happy-looking Western men and very young Thai girls. This is the ugliest face of Thai prostitution. It often involves children. The photographs were no accident. They were advertisements.

In brothels girls are segregated by age. Those younger than eighteen are on one side of the room; those older than eighteen are on the other. Men, especially Western men, it seems, like little girls and the younger a girl, the more popular and successful she tends to be. Bobby told me that when it was mentioned in passing that the girl he bought in Bangkok was twenty-one, she objected vehemently, even tearfully. She was only eighteen, she swore to Bobby. He didn't care; the pimp shrugged. But to the girl it was more than a matter of vanity. Thai prostitutes, like international gymnasts, have brief, early careers.

Late the afternoon of my first day in Thailand, I wandered through the shops and fashionable hotels along Rama

IV Road. Perhaps it was just that I was now attuned, but everywhere I saw Bangkok odd couples. Sometimes they walked hand in hand, sometimes arm in arm; sometimes they seemed afraid to touch, like seventh graders on their first date. And neither that day nor any day did I ever see anyone smirk, raise an eyebrow, or look askance even when the difference in ages was obscene. If this was not considered normal, it was at least routine.

That evening I ate an early dinner in the lovely garden of the stylish J'it Pochana Restaurant, and they were all around me. There was a very elegant and well-dressed Thai woman of about thirty-five with a drunken German man who nodded over his food and sneered at her. I could not figure out their relationship. She did not fit the stereotype, but neither did she seem a wife or secretary. There was a good-looking young Australian fellow trying earnestly to talk to his Thai girlfriend. He was not getting very far. There was a fat, handsome American with several gold rings, a brandy snifter in one hand and a huge cigar in the other. The little girl across the table from him played with the straw in her Coke. When they left, she nearly fell off her spike heels.

Back at the hotel, an international soccer match was on the lobby television. They were all sitting there together: the Arabs, the Aussies, the Europeans, the one African, even the Japanese. Pass the bean dip, please. Across the way all of their girlfriends were gathered around one big table in the coffee shop. I watched them. I looked at them. I wonder if they were good spellers, because that is what Asian women had always been to me: pretty, passive little women who followed the rules and won spelling bees. I thought sitting there in that coffee shop watching this strange, interesting little community of prostitutes how seldom I had looked at Asian women's faces. That had all changed very recently—not only because of my trip, but because at home I had found myself suddenly and dramatically thrust into the life of a young Korean woman who seemed hell-bent on not being typical, and was making me reexamine the prejudices I didn't know I had.

I changed into my bathing suit and robe and went down for a swim. The Aussie from the night before was doing slow, tortured laps, while his girlfriend sat at the edge of the pool. He stopped every few minutes and bobbed beside her talking confidentially. I dried off, ordered a Singha, put my feet up, reminded myself several times that I was on vacation and told myself that I was having fun. But when I opened the *Bangkok Post,* the first story I saw was about a police raid that had freed girls held in white slavery. Those under sixteen years of age were in government custody.

Bangkok was getting me down. I decided to leave the next day on the overnight train through the mountains to Chiang Mai, the capital of the north. It was on the train that I met Suzanne Schmidt, a German filmmaker who had been interviewing bar girls for a documentary on prostitution. She had been impressed by their candor and refusal to justify, excuse, or rationalize. I asked her if they are all great actresses. "Oh, no, not at all."

"But they can't be sincere—"

"Oh, yes, I think so. They are polite to us; they are polite to each other. They wish to please. They are gracious hostesses who want their guests to be at ease and happy."

"As hostesses, yes, but as lovers—"

"They understand affection differently. Perhaps it is Buddhism. They see all relationships, not just this one, as transitory. They have fewer expectations than we do."

On the same train I met a social-services agency worker who strongly disagreed. (She asked not to be identified.) She had lived in Southeast Asia for nearly twenty years and had two adopted Laotian children, both now teenage girls. "They (Thai girlfriends) are very sad girls. They do not want this. It is forced upon them. Many are too poor and ignorant to have any choice. If you knew some of the things I have seen. There have been fires, and afterward they find the girls chained to their beds."

"Still, many seem to function quite freely."

"For many it's their only chance."

"Chance for what?"

"Chance to make money, to stay in fancy hotels, eat in fancy restaurants, buy clothes, buy cheap jewelry—these can be very young girls—even have a Westerner fall in love with them and take them away."

"Does that happen?"

"Sure, and someone wins the lottery every day."

All of this was on my mind a week later when I had dinner with Bobby Quinn and Sahli. Before Sahli crossed her arms and left, I had asked Bobby what was wrong with the girl in Bangkok. "Nothing, really. She is a wonderful girl. Do anything for me, but it was dark in there, and I was nervous. I don't know. She's a little chunky. Sometimes I kid her and say I'll trade her in at 'Happy Days'—that's the name of the massage parlor—but—"

"Could you do that?"

"Oh, yeah, but she gets all upset, says 'No! No! No!' She doesn't want to go back. So"—there was a long pause—"besides, she has a kid, and she doesn't want to go to Alaska."

"Go to Alaska? Did you ask her to?"

"We talked about it. I showed her my pictures." He produced a battered envelope, twenty-four shots of bleak, treeless landscape, his boat, his friends, the town, a buddy's cabin that looked a little like a clubhouse adolescents might have built, and some aerial views.

"Most of the women there have been around the block a few times. Been around a few blocks. You can go to Anchorage and get a woman. Go to Seattle. Sure would be nice to have a woman out there."

"How about Sahli?"

"Yeah. She says she'll go."

"You asked her?"

"Yeah."

The next morning when I got into the front seat of the old Nissan Cedric with the guide, Roger Hodges and his wife Namor were already in the back. We were off for a day of touring northern Thailand, flirting with the Golden Triangle, visiting a Meo tribe village, watching a staged elephant show high in the rugged teak forests, stopping at an experimental orchid farm. There had been just enough rumors of guerrilla ambushes and drug-war skirmishes in the area to add spice if not real peril to our excursion.

Roger was a pleasant, circumspect Australian who folded his long legs before him and sank deep in the seat. I had no idea of his height until we got out sometime later. He and I chatted while his wife, who was Thai, talked to the guide.

In the course of the conversation, I said that I did not like Bangkok very much. Roger liked it. "Canberra," he said by way of explanation, "is a city of bureaucrats. Quiet . . . unexciting." He worked as a shipping clerk there. This was his sixth trip to Thailand. On his first he met his wife. On his third he married her. Now he had brought her back to visit her family and friends. He himself was a great admirer of Thailand, its people, its natural beauty, its culture, its history. "Thailand has been here for two and a half thousand years, and we in the West think we have culture. It is the land of the free." (This is a title claimed by Thailand because, unlike most of its neighbors, it was never colonized.) "I'll tell you, if there was ever a war, I would want to be on Thailand's side. The Thais never give up."

I was not entirely sure Roger knew what he was talking about, but I liked him. He was a retiring, homely man in his early thirties who didn't always know where to put his hands, especially when I took a picture of his wife and him in front of a little waterfall we had stopped to explore. Then she was off with the guide, stepping from stone to stone headed upstream.

Roger and I took off our shoes and cooled our feet. Yes, she quite liked Canberra. There were other Thai girls there she saw. She spoke some English; he spoke a little Thai. "But it is a very difficult language. There are forty-seven letters, but only one vowel. Then there are ten more letters that are used only in ceremonial words. And there are no prepositions."

Namor cavorted on the rocks above, mugged for us, called out in a screechy voice. She was cute, but not pretty. She still wore the bright T-shirt and tight jeans that are the uniform of the Thai girlfriend, but she had abandoned the high heels in favor of more sensible sneakers.

"She is a very innocent creature," said Roger, watching her bemused. "By that I mean without inhibitions, very natural. She has no sense of Western morality, you see." I was a little surprised by his paternalistic tone. "I have only to feed her twenty-four hours a day. She eats constantly." Later, on the way back to the car, she raced ahead to a food stand. "See?" He smiled.

That evening, my last in Chiang Mai, I had drinks with Bobby Quinn again and told him about Roger and Namor. Then, late the next afternoon as I was hurrying to catch the overnight back to Bangkok, baggage in hand, I saw Sahli coming down the platform toward me. We were both very happy to see each other, as if we were old friends or more. We were tempted to embrace, but both of us thought better of it at the last moment.

"Sahli," I said, "what in the world are you doing here?"

"Bobby." She pointed to the train and held up eight fingers.

"Bobby's on the train?" I said. "He's leaving Chiang Mai? But why?"

That was a question she couldn't negotiate. She shrugged and smiled. We bowed, giggled, again resisted the temptation to touch each other, and parted. I turned to watch her go, and she turned once, too.

After I got settled, and we were under way, I found Bobby in car eight and bought him a beer. I was surprised that he was on the train because he had not intended to leave for two or three more days. But things had changed. Bobby had searched out Roger and Namor, and the two couples had spent the day together. Roger had had some very specific advice: "Spend as much time together as possible. Then go home. Write letters. Give it some time. Come for another visit. Then make up your mind."

Bobby was on his way to Bangkok to see if he could get a visa extension. Both he and Sahli knew that the odds were slim, but . . . he imagined her out on the crab boat with him. Perhaps she could cook. They had lain in the dark and talked. She seemed willing. Still, she was so quiet, so shy. He wished she were more outgoing, like Roger's wife.

That evening I stopped to talk to an American woman in my car. She was a linguist from San Jose, California, who had lived fifteen years in southeast Asia and taught the last two at the University of Chiang Mai. I repeated what Roger had told me about the Thai language. She smiled and shook her head. It was all wrong. There are many vowels and, of course, there are prepositions.

In Bangkok the next morning Bobby and I shared a cab. He gave the address of his old hotel.

"What about the girl there?" I asked.

"I don't know. I don't much want to be with her after Sahli, but I don't want to hurt her feelings." He paused. "I could give her to you. Do you want her?"

"Sure. I'll give you two Mickey Mantles and a Whitey Ford for her." We both laughed. "No, since I leave tomorrow, I don't want to blow it. Then I couldn't be smug about all of this." And I realized that I was apologizing once again for not having taken part in Thailand's carnal circus.

Across the narrow street from my new hotel was a strip

joint. Girls with waist-length hair and tight skirts sat at the open-air bar out front. When any potential customer passed, they stopped talking, leered, postured, licked their lips, winked, and whistled. They reminded me of Loop construction workers on their lunch break.

All day I wandered through Bangkok's shops and bazaars, its Indian market and vast Chinatown. Officially I was shopping. Actually I was thinking about Bobby and Sahli and Roger Hodges and Namor and the Korean woman back home. About the tiny schoolchildren I had seen everywhere who all wore blue slacks or skirts, crisp white shirts, and carried black satchels. About the rooms full of chanting monks in soft saffron robes and the Thai pirates who preyed upon refugees. About the giggling Thai kids who played Motown tunes as the train from Chiang Mai climbed into the mountains and the obnoxious, funny teenagers who shared a bottle of Thai whiskey and leaned screaming from the train windows; they reminded me of my old high school crowd. About every pretty girl I had seen with an ugly man. About the hundreds of cabs that had honked at me and the dozens of people who had stepped into my path and asked, "Where you go, man?" About the woman who had crossed the street from her house to squat beside me when I sat in the shade by a stream and touch my leg and ask, "I love you?"

I was up at dawn. I rode the city bus to the airport because it cost much less than a cab. It was Sunday, and neither the bus nor the streets were crowded. Across the aisle from me, a girl slept. She held a brochure in her hand. On it I could read in big red letters "Sexy Gal." There was a snapshot of a girl posing one hand behind her head a la Marilyn Monroe. The sleeping girl's hair had fallen forward so that I could not tell if she was the girl in the photo. I watched her. I wondered if she was up very early or very late. I suspected very late. Now that I looked, she was wearing white leather slacks and high heels. She was carrying a quite expensive leather purse. On it, I suddenly realized, were emblazoned dozens of little Elmos.

When I got off the bus, she was still asleep.

6

• • •

LOOKING FOR PETER

WHEN I CAME IN the door, Lydia was sitting on the couch with her arms crossed. "Hi," I said, a bit surprised.

"There's a message for you."

"Okay. Has Art been out?" I asked.

"He can wait."

I put my briefcase on the dining-room table and went into the kitchen, punched the button.

"Pete. It's Tanya Kim. Uh, Lisa tested positive for heroin. It was a private autopsy, and my dad had it sealed, so no one knows this, but I decided you should. Please keep it confidential. 'Bye." I rewound the tape and listened for the time of the call. Right in the middle of the day, when she could be fairly certain I would not be home. Obviously she did not want to talk about this.

I turned around, and Lydia was standing in the doorway arms still crossed. "What the hell is that all about?"

"Lisa Kim. Look, I know that sounded bad, but—"

"I thought Lisa Kim was dead," she said pointedly.

"That was her sister on the phone."

"What is her sister doing calling you? I don't understand. Are you seeing her sister now?"

"No, no. I ran into her. I just ran into her at Café Express a week ago Saturday. We had a cup of coffee. It's kind of fascinating, really. Tanya feels—"

"It's not fascinating. It's not at all fascinating. It's a little sick, if you ask me. I think you're obsessed. How in God's name do you even know her sister, anyway?"

She'd nailed me. She had me dead to rights.

"Why would she recognize you? Why would *you* recognize *her*? Do you know her?"

I was trapped. "I went to the funeral," I said quietly.

"Oh Jesus." Lydia sank down at the kitchen table and put her head in her hands. "Why are you involving yourself in these peoples' lives, for God's sake?"

"I'm not involving—"

"And what about *our* lives? What's happened to *our* lives?"

I might have said, "I thought you didn't want lives together. Wasn't that the deal? 'An alliance rather than a marriage' didn't you once say?" But instead I said, "I know; I've been a little preoccupied."

"A little, for Chrissake? You forgot my birthday. You've taken how many days off from work now? You left your wallet in the avocados in the grocery store and didn't even know it until they called you. You lost your car for two days; how can you lose a car? And what's this about heroin? And tell me this: What's 'I thought you should know.' Why should you know, for God's sake? Why should you know? Were you having a relationship with this woman? I mean, did you know her before this accident for Chrissake? Were you chasing her or something?"

"Chasing her?"

"Yes, chasing her, and you're still chasing her. She's dead and you're still chasing her."

"Me?"

I call Art "the dog who walks himself" because he doesn't need a leash; he follows right on my heel wherever I go even through crowds of people or heavy traffic, even like that night for miles and miles. I started off thinking about, fuming about, fretting about Lydia, about her using the word "relationship" rather than "affair" out of habit, because "affair" would suggest the illicit, and back in the day Lydia had insisted that no real relationship, no matter how brief, could be illicit. When I had first met Lydia, she had been promiscuous as a matter of principle and had once boasted that she had slept with people of every race and twenty-four nationalities as if she were collecting postage or passport stamps. For a while she would ask people at parties if they knew any good-looking Egyptians or Surinamese. I found all of this amusing and even titillating, as if her flouting of convention reflected well on me as her companion. For a couple of years when we first got together, she would react to occasions when she found herself feeling uncomfortably close to me by going right out and sleeping with someone else. These liaisons never bothered me much because they were almost always one-night stands.

Later on in my walk that night, I started thinking about Lisa. Annie Pritchard had been telling the truth; Lisa Kim had been high on heroin. Damn. Two loose ends had come together. Now I knew what I had to do next. Halfway through the walk, I stopped and bought a pack of cigarettes.

On an April day my afternoon classes were canceled because of a motivational speaker. I hate motivational speakers and often complain about the money and time we waste on them. This time I decided on a more subversive form of protest than my usual irate voice-mail or indignant e-mail. The Cubs had been rained out the day before and were playing a doubleheader starting at noon. The Internet said the weather would be chilly but sunny, so by 11:00 I had taken the afternoon off and contacted Officer Lotts, who was working four to midnight and would be delighted to join me for game one at least.

"Section 242?" he asked.

Section 242 is a terrace of seats down the right-field line that looks back on the field and gets a lot of spring sun. The seats are reserved, but no one checks your ticket especially on a May weekday afternoon. Steve was reading the *New York Times* with his backpack on his lap when I got there in the second inning. I pointed at the backpack. "Armed?"

"Of course."

We were happy to be in the sun. People who weren't in it froze. We talked Cubs and politics expressing in our liberal, noodle-headed way that the Republicans are all self-serving nitwits. Steve told me about a big drug bust he had been part of. We needed a list of things to talk about; we'd rarely been together without Carolyn, and weren't close enough friends to be comfortable not talking. I used the drug bust as a segue into the question I really wanted to ask him: "What if I knew a bartender who was selling drugs?"

"What if you knew one who wasn't?"

I told him that I was talking about heroin, and he got a little more interested, so I told him the heroin might have led to someone's death.

He pulled back and looked at me. "This isn't about that Korean chick, is it?"

"Well, yes."

"I think you've got a bit of a postmortem crush going here."

"What if this guy sold her heroin and she drove into a pole and killed herself?"

"What do you want to know?"

"Could you do anything?"

"You mean charge him?" He asked me if there were witnesses to the sale or to her using the drugs. He asked if she had any previous drug offenses. When I answered no, he said, "Pete, there's nothing there."

"Okay. Suppose there are witnesses. Suppose I buy drugs from him and then testify against him."

"He said, she said. Maybe you have a grudge against him. In fact, you *do* have a grudge against him. Besides—"

"Besides what?" I asked.

"Never mind."

"You mean it's small potatoes."

"I mean, why are you doin' this shit, Pete?"

"Doing *what* shit?"

"You know exactly what I'm talking about. If this girl was using big drugs like that, you don't want to have any part of it. There are bad people in the drug business. Bad people. You can get hurt. You can get killed, for Chrissake."

I told him that I knew all of that. I told him I wouldn't take chances.

"You're already taking chances," he said. "You're taking chances with your job; you got a cop coming to your school, for Chrissake. You're taking chances with Lydia."

"What does that mean?" I asked.

"Lydia's worried about you," he said.

"Have you been talking to Lydia? What the hell's going on?"

"She's my friend, too, you know. And she's concerned."

"Look Steve, Lydia thinks I'm playing a game . . ."

"Well, are you?"

"No, I'm not," I said evenly. "Look, I saw a person die. It affected me. I know you see people die all the time, but I don't. This has made me think about things."

"I'm sure it has," he said less forcefully. "I know it has."

"And all I get from you guys is that I'm playing a game or acting irresponsibly or being self-indulgent or juvenile. I don't think I'm doing or being any of that, and I'm tired of being patronized. I might be being responsible about something—morally responsible—for the first time in my life. And what's everyone so worried about? Let me follow this thing. Let me do what I need to do, okay?"

That left us in an awkward place, but the first game was just ending (the Cubs won to our surprise and mild delight), and Steve went to work. He walked away but came back to say, "Listen, we're going to have a celebration at Davis Street on June third for Wendy and Carolyn."

"What are we celebrating?"

"You didn't hear? Wendy really did it," he said. "She quit."

"No kidding? And Caro, she getting married?"

"No." The doctor had said he wanted to see other women, so Carolyn dumped him. No, the party was because she'd been hired as a vice president and general counsel of a big hospital and was taking the summer off to go to Europe with Wendy before she started.

"No kidding."

"Write it down," he said. "June third."

Steve Lotts and Carolyn O'Connor had been friends since childhood, and for some years best friends, but they had never been lovers. Apparently, not even once. In fact, when you asked what you thought would be the logical questions ("Since you two are so close, haven't you ever . . . ?" "Why don't you two just . . . ?"), they both answered "no" so immediately, so dismissively, so absolutely that you thought you must have suggested something sordid and awful like incest. Personally, I thought that that was really the answer; in the world of urban singles, they had become each other's family. They had lived together and traveled together (they were both scuba divers), and they did lots of things family members do for each other: They went to weddings, funerals, and emergency rooms together, they brought each other food and magazines when they were sick, they understood each other's limits, tastes, and taboos, they took each other out on their birthdays for fancy lunches and at Christmastime for a fancier brunch at the Drake Hotel, and they bought each other elaborate, thoughtful presents. Now you have two questions, I know. No, neither of them was gay, at least as far as I knew; they'd each had several important relationships that just hadn't lasted. And why if they could do these things for each other, couldn't they do them for a mate? I did not know the answer to that other than to say again, love is hard.

The grandstands were now in total shade, and I was getting chilled, but there were guys in the bleachers in shirtsleeves, so I bought a second ticket (they are half price on weekdays in April) for game two and sat out there in the sun. When we were in high school and college, my friends and I would sit in the bleachers often. We'd ride our bikes to the park, chain them to no parking signs, buy bleacher tickets, hot dogs, and Cokes all for five bucks a head, then ride home. If it was hot, we'd stop at Chase Street and jump into Lake Michigan off the rocks.

It was about the same, and yet it wasn't, like Volkswagens; the bleachers got fashionable and expensive. The clientele were all young people strutting, posing, being self-consciously jocular or mysterious or intense. I watched them as if through bulletproof glass and wondered if I had ever looked quite so silly. I must have. I'd spent too much time in the place not to have looked silly some of it.

The very first time was when I was eleven, and Wrigley Field now evokes in me a certain sadness for times past, people lost, other people dead. When he was a kid, Bill Veeck helped plant the ivy on the walls, and as an old man after he'd sold the White Sox, he came back here for a few summers and sat in the first row of the centerfield bleachers. Anyone could sit beside him if there was a seat, and I did a time or two. Bill Veeck with an ashtray built into his wooden leg wheezing and coughing. He'd stopped smoking by then, but he could see what was going to kill him from a long way off. Kennedy couldn't. He never heard of Lee Harvey Oswald. He never heard of Jack Ruby or Jim Garrison or Lieutenant William Calley or Chappaquiddick Island or "one small step for a man" or young Bill Clinton waiting on the White House lawn to shake the president's hand and change his own life forever.

Many of us, most of us I suppose, never know what hits us, never know this critical fact about our own lives: how we die. Lisa Kim certainly didn't, certainly never heard of me and here she was causing all this interesting trouble in my life. And it was trouble, and it was interesting. Steve Lotts and I had never had a real conversation like that in all our lives. And Lydia, what was she so concerned about, and why was I not concerned that she was? Had I felt that she was taking me for granted? But wasn't that what she was supposed to do? Wasn't that part of our contract? And had that contract changed without my noticing it? Or maybe it was I who had changed it; otherwise why would I resent being taken for granted? No, that wasn't it at all. I had taken myself for granted. That was it; it had been going on for a long time, and somehow in the process, several years of my life had slipped away. I could barely remember anything about them that would distinguish one from another. The realization that I had allowed this to happen to myself gave me a chill, and I shivered.

I touched my fingers to my face. It was a signal to myself that I had begun to use, a reminder that I was alive. My skin touching my skin. Warm fingers on cool flesh. Cold fingers on warm cheek. I had made a decision to live every day not as if it were my last day, but as if it were my only day; not so that I would remember it in a year or even in a month, but so that at the end of it when I lay down at night, I could say that I had not wasted it, not sleepwalked through it, that I had lived it.

The guy in front of me jumped up, turned around, and gave me a high five. The Cubs had won the second game. No one present was able to recall the last time they had swept a doubleheader.

Peter Carey lived in a one-bedroom apartment in a shabby building on an uptown block that hadn't been stately in a long time. He shopped in a convenience store on Clark Street (Campbell's Bean with Bacon Soup, Skippy peanut butter, and a six-pack of Heineken. I sat in my car across the street with a pair of binoculars.) and watched TV late into the night; judging from how rapidly the images flickered on his living-room ceiling, I guessed MTV. The next time I sat down at the bar, he recognized me.

"Hey, you're Lisa's friend."

"Yes. No, we weren't personal friends. Actually I'm a writer, and I was doing a piece on her."

"She that big?"

"Well, it was on a bunch of young Chicago actors. She was just one of them."

"Oh, she was an actor, all right."

Two days later, I asked him what he meant by that.

"She was always onstage," he said. "Everything was a performance. Everything. A soap opera. No, that doesn't do her justice. She was like a Mamet play, maybe, something dark and clever, brainy."

Another time I bought him a beer, and he sat beside me at the bar at the end of his shift to drink it. "You ever go with a really beautiful woman? I mean, a Lisa Kim?" he asked me.

"No, not really."

"Don't. Believe me, it isn't worth it. It's like they're doing you a favor, you know? It's like they allow you to make love to them. Sex with a beautiful woman is not a participatory event. For them, I mean. You do all the work. You get to worship her. It sucks. Actually, it doesn't suck. Rule Number 1: Beautiful women don't give head. Like Lisa—I'll tell you something just fucking nuts; she use to dangle her head over the edge of the bed backward, so I couldn't even see her face. So I'm thinking, what the hell is she doing? Then I figure it out. She's looking at herself. She's fucking looking at herself upside down with her hair hanging down to the floor in the mirror on the closet door. She had to have set it up, too; planned it, moved the door just right, got in just the right place on the bed. I'm telling you, it was fucking crazy. Here I am boinking away, and she's staring at herself." He shook his head. "No, give me a chick who's a little rough around the edges any day. I'm with Springsteen on that one."

When I went out to my car, I listened to the little tape recorder I'd hidden in my jacket pocket. It got every word. A few days later, I went to Paddy Shea's right from school. The bar was empty, and Peter Carey was alone.

"Hey," he said, "how you doing?"

"Good," I said. "Guinness, please." When he brought it, I said, "You know Annie Pritchard?"

"Sure, I know Annie. Another friend of Lisa's. How's she doing?"

"Good. She said maybe you could help me out."

"Yeah?"

"Yeah. I'm interested in doing some kind of special partying."

The phone rang, and he went to answer it. I felt for the tape recorder in my pocket. It was warm and moving.

"Special partying," he said when he came back. "What's that mean, exactly? Drugs?"

I wrote the word in the margin of the sports page and turned it toward him. I said it out loud. He looked at it, and then looked at me. "You're full of surprises," he said. "Listen pal, I don't do anything with drugs."

"I know," I said. "I know you don't; Annie told me that, but she said you might know someone who knows someone."

"I don't know anyone who knows anyone."

"Problem is, neither do I, and I gotta get this stuff—don't ask why—and I'm willing to pay good money to get it," I said.

"I don't know no one who knows no one." He walked away. For the next week, he didn't speak to me or make eye contact, and I was sure I'd lost him.

"Shit," I thought.

Then one day he said out of nowhere, "What kind of cigarettes do you smoke?"

I pointed to the pack in front of me.

"You ever smoke cigarettes in a hard pack?"

"No." I thought it an odd question.

"Go buy yourself a hard pack of Virginia Slims. Put three hundred bucks in twenties in it. Leave it on the bar tomorrow afternoon."

I did it. I read my paper, drank my beer, and walked out leaving the tip and the cigarette box on the bar. I came back the next day and waited over an hour. I had to go to the bathroom and turn my tape over. I was wet under my arms. Finally I said, "Do you have something for me?"

"Nope," he answered.

"What do you mean, 'Nope'?"

"I mean I don't have anything for you," he said.

"You want me to come back tomorrow?" I asked.

"Nope. I won't have anything then, either. I told you: I'm not a drug dealer." He smiled at me.

"You are a drug dealer. You sold Lisa Kim drugs."

"I thought that's what this might be about. You taping this, maybe? Let me get good and close and say this loud and clear. Ready? I am not a drug dealer. I did not sell Lisa Kim drugs. I did not give Lisa Kim drugs. I do not do drugs."

"Then give me my money back," I said.

"Nope."

"What do you mean, 'Nope'?"

"I'm not going to give you your money back," he said.

"You're kidding. You're a thief," I said.

"There you go. I'm a thief, but I'm not a drug dealer, and now you know the difference. It's a cheap lesson, really, and an important one for a guy like you. Might save your life someday. You don't want to go fucking around with those guys. Now I think it's time for you to go, and don't come back, either. You're getting to be a real pain in the ass."

There was nothing to say. I gathered my change and headed for the door. His last words to me were, "I thought the Virginia Slims box was a particularly nice touch, didn't you?"

7

. . .

THE LONG, COLD SPRING

HE PETER CAREY debacle was embarrassing, but not as much as I would have imagined. It was as if I had plumbed the depths of humiliation, and they weren't all that deep. Besides, like Brueghel's Icarus falling into the sea, no one even seemed to notice, and since I had something of a head of steam, a couple of days later I read over the notes I'd made on Annie Pritchard and took Art for another long walk. The more I thought about it, the more I came to feel that she had not known that Lisa was using heroin before we met. She might have discerned it, she might have deduced it, but she didn't know it, and her pretending to proved to me only that she didn't, and indicated she didn't even suspect it. She wanted to never be surprised by anything, but she was covering; and if she didn't know or at least suspect, then why not? She was the kind of person who would suspect, maybe know, something even if it were not true. Did this mean Lisa wasn't using heroin? But we knew that she was.

I went home and wrote Tanya:

> I am trying to find out who gave Lisa the drugs because I think that person was at least partly responsible for her death, but I've hit a dead end. Can you shed any light on this at all? Do you know of any friends or acquaintances, old or new, who might have given her the stuff? Do you know of anything curious or suspicious that took place in the last weeks or months of her life?
>
> Tanya, I know Lisa was difficult, and I know you have mixed feelings about her (I do, too), but I don't believe she should have died. Help me if you can.

It was Memorial Day weekend, and Art and I drove around the lake to my family's summer home. It's an old cottage built in 1908 on a high dune a quarter mile from and overlooking Lake Michigan near South Haven, Michigan. My grandfather, who was a Presbyterian minister and moved frequently in his career, bought it in 1926 and returned to it each summer. My father, who was also a minister and who also moved frequently, bought it from my grandfather. My mother still spends her summers there. My brother and sister-in-law spend vacations there, too.

It is a simple house that is beautiful in its simplicity. Built on a hilltop out of cement blocks made with the sand dug to lay the foundation and molded on the site, the house is a thirty-foot square that is cut in half. One half is a living room, and the other is cut in half again into two bedrooms that no one sleeps in. This blockhouse is surrounded on all sides by a continuous screened porch (continuous except in one rear corner where two small side by side bathrooms are located) that is six feet wide on the three sides used for sleeping and twelve feet wide on the one used for living. There's a fireplace and a skylight in the living room, a peaked roof made of exposed cedar shakes hand cut on the property from trees felled to clear the lot a hundred years ago, and a lower level beneath the wide porch that consists of a kitchen, a dining room, and a study all in a row with windows on three sides.

I had come to open the cottage for the season. I had come alone; it was a long, cold spring, and Lydia had looked at the weather forecast and decided to stay home. Just as well; I needed some time to think about Lydia and me. Of course I didn't do it. In fact, I avoided doing it all weekend long.

I had come to this place, this summer village, every summer of my life; it's the closest thing to true home for me. It is where I know Carolyn O'Connor and Steve Lotts from, and half a dozen important people in my life. Most people there know me and some like me; it is the place where I don't need to explain very much. Once, years ago, during that summer I spent in England, I dragged David Lehman down to Bournemouth on a hot weekend. I did not know why until I got there, until I walked out to the end of the long town pier late at night, stood with my back to the land listening to two German guys playing a guitar and singing, and realized that I'd come to look at Lake Michigan.

It was cool and drizzly, but I worked hard and kept warm. I washed and cleaned the fridge and all the kitchen cabinets, wiping away a winter's worth of dust and mouse droppings, swept and scrubbed the tile floors on my hands and knees, washed windows, and when the porch had dried, I rolled out rugs, moved furniture, set up beds, and lugged mattresses.

By late afternoon the weather had begun to clear. I put on a heavy sweater and a windbreaker, pulled up a big wicker chair to watch the sun play on the lake and drank a Belgian beer I had brought for the occasion. I was thinking about my father. He always took his vacation the month of August, and he worked every day of it painting, repairing, or building. We would say, "Jeez, Dad, some vacation." But he would always say something about how working with his hands was therapy for him because he never got to do it. His one indulgence was a plunge into the lake just before dinner, just at this time of day. He would soap his body all over and swim hard out a hundred yards and back. Sometimes I went with him.

Thinking there might be a sunset, I took Art down to the beach. Despite the late sunshine, the air was cold and the water colder. It would be weeks before anyone would swim in this lake. Even Art was content to wrestle a stick on the sand. We headed along the shore. O'Connor's cottage was brightly lighted and full of people. Some of them were having drinks on the front deck in heavy sweaters and jackets. Someone called my name. It was Carolyn. She leaned over the railing to speak to me. "Where's Lydia?"

"She didn't come. I'm just opening up the cottage."

"We're having a wine tasting. Come join us."

"Who's here?"

"Bunch of people I brought up from the city. You know some of them. Let me get you a glass."

I probably should have known that these people were going to piss me off because my mood had soured as the day had waned, and I was feeling a bit like Ishmael, ready to step into the street and knock people's hats off, but I was enticed by the light and the warmth of the house and by the wine, as well. I stood at the back of the deck and watched the sun go down. I went inside by the fire. A wry, slow-talking Hoosier I'd enjoyed a time or two in the past seemed to be performing tonight. I stood outside a group of people who kept turning their shoulders to me. Their gaiety seemed artificial, their wit acrid and sarcastic. I didn't like it.

I went into the kitchen. There was a little architect I vaguely knew sitting on the counter, one leg folded beneath him and a sweater tied loosely around his neck. He seemed to be with Carolyn. He was giving her and two other women instructions on how to drink wine. "Let's see if it has legs," he said. They all held their oversized glasses up to the light and swished the wine around in them.

"Now, the bouquet," he said. He held his glass beneath his nose and fanned the scent toward himself, then plunged his nose in. The others imitated him.

"Christ," I thought. I went out, found Art by the fire, put my glass down, and let myself out the front door. It closed and then opened again behind me.

"Pete?" It was Carolyn.

"Sorry," I said, "I'm in a shitty mood."

"We're going to have some dinner later," she said.

"No thanks."

"You okay?"

"I'm okay." I went home and opened a bottle of red wine of my own. I cooked some spaghetti carbonara thinking about Carolyn. I was disappointed in her; what was she doing with that prissy little phony? I was disappointed in myself. Why was I so black? I built a big fire, ate in front of it, finished the wine, and spent the rest of the evening listening to music and reading. I slept on the porch in the open air beneath lots of quilts and blankets. The next morning I lay in bed on the porch with Art curled beside me, reading for an hour, then took a very hot shower and started working. The hard work was done, and the urgency was gone. I played tunes and took my time. It was sunny and I worked outside. I raked leaves, swept the walks, swept and washed down the patio, put the patio furniture out. In the afternoon I moved inside. My mother had asked me to clean out my dad's old storage closet, which we had all been avoiding since his death. It was stuffed with boxes, tools, and lots of personal junk, so I turned the Cubs game on the radio and opened the door.

I thought it would be hard, but it wasn't hard. It was nice. It was a lot like seeing him again. And there was all kinds of stuff in there: the world's oldest chain saw, a World War I army helmet with mouse-eaten netting inside, three of the mice who had eaten it (one mummified and two skeletons), a wooden Don Budge tennis racket with a triangular open-ing in the neck (for aerodynamic effect? whip action?), an ancient unworn pair of tennis shoes still in their box, never even laced, pristine and brittle after however many Michigan winters, a white enamel bedpan connected somehow to my grandmother by a famous story I can't remember, two moth-eaten squirrels stuffed and mounted on a shellacked tree branch. There was a pint of cherry vodka. There were about thirty mason jars of nails, screws, nuts, bolts and washers all neatly sorted and labeled, proving the irrelevance of saving things; I threw them all away. There were six plastic fireman hats purchased for some silliness or other, worn once, stacked and stuck away and four handmade coffee mugs wrapped in the *South Haven Tribune* dated August 1956; a gift never given? "And why not?" I wondered. There was a treasure trove of tools: hammers, screwdrivers, box wrenches, monkey wrenches, pliers, vise grips, chisels, a hand drill, a hacksaw, a level, and a rusted tape measure. And at the very back of the top shelf against the wall and wrapped in a single fold of canvas was a .22 caliber rifle with two boxes of cartridges. This last item quite surprised me; who could have put it there? My grandfather? One of my uncles? Surely not my father who had been so opposed to violence his whole life. But if he did not put it there, at least he had left it there, and against what? Raccoons? Nazis during the war? Angry blacks from Detroit or the South Side of Chicago? Intruders in the night? What secret fears had occupied his heart as he lay here in the dark?

I took the gun out and dusted it off. It seemed brand-new, and I wondered if it had ever been fired. I opened both boxes of shells. None seemed to be missing. I attached the barrel with its single screw. I loaded the rifle. I sat on the front porch and held it across my knees. I cocked it, held the stock between my feet, and put the barrel in my mouth. I tasted the hard, cold metal. I thought of all the people for whom this had been life's final sensation. I thought again, as I had so often since Lisa Kim, of all the things that lay within my power to do, including this one. I leaned it against the doorjamb and from time to time that afternoon I walked past it. It was a little exciting to see it sitting there so still and lethal.

I went into town and bought a piece of trout, a couple of red-skinned potatoes, some locally grown asparagus and a bottle of white wine, grilled the fish and asparagus, boiled the potatoes, drank the wine, and read myself to sleep, the rifle still leaning in the doorway. The next day, before I locked the cottage and drove back into the city, I unloaded the gun, took it apart, and put it back where I had found it. I couldn't think of what else to do with it.

Lydia was sitting on the couch again Tuesday evening when I came into our apartment from walking Art after work. No radio, no television, no magazine, catalog, or book. Her arms were crossed. "Would you mind telling me what's going on around here?" she asked. I recognized Lisa's letter lying on the couch beside her and felt my hip pocket; I must have taken it out with my wallet and left it on my dresser. I could think of nothing to say perhaps because I did not *know* what was going on. Fortunately, the questions that Lydia asked me were all rhetorical and did not require responses.

"You were screwing the Korean chick, weren't you?" she said. "In fact, you were with her that night. That's why you were late. You were following her. You were in love with her."

"No, no," I finally sputtered.

"No, no?" And with that she produced her coup de grâce: There in her hand was another letter, the one I had recently sent to Tanya Kim. I would later find when I picked up the envelope from the floor that it was stamped RETURN TO SENDER; I had omitted the street name. (I am a little embarrassed to admit this, but I sent it again to the right address the next day.) The letter had been opened, and now Lydia unfolded it and read, "'I know you have mixed feelings about her (I do, too).' For God's sake, Pete, why do you have any feelings about her at all?"

I probably should have said something right then, but what was I to tell her: the truth? Well, you see, I've become hopelessly entangled in the life of a dead woman I never met although I do know her parents, her sisters, her old friends and lovers, and I have stalked her through letters and year-books and school hallways, and I have made love to her in my dreams. It seemed unlikely that Lydia would respond positively to candor. Besides, she went on to say, "And if you weren't screwing her, if this is all just . . . God, I don't even want to think about that. That would be too weird."

So the truth was out of the question, which left only the untruth, and I just didn't have the energy to start lying, so I didn't say much of anything. Besides, I was pretty sure that she would blow sky-high, and that there was nothing I could do to stop it. You see, Lydia was heavily armed with self-protective devices. Early in our relationship, one had been her aversion to commitment, but later another was commitment itself. When we got back from Mexico, signed a lease together, and opened a joint bank account, she made an announcement (and that's what it was, an announcement) that if I ever cheated on her, she would pack her bags, leave that day, and never look back. So what happened next was quite unexpected.

Lydia crossed her arms again and turned away to look out the window. Then she turned back. "Look, Pete, none of that matters. What does matter is that there's something go-ing on with us. I feel like I'm standing on the shore and you're going out to sea and all I can do is just watch."

"Well," I said, a bit uncomfortable with her sudden famil-iarity, "what about ships passing in the night?"

"What do you mean?"

Once when it was I who was feeling insecure, I told Lydia that I felt like we were ships passing in the night, and she said, "That's my definition of a perfect relationship: ships passing in the night."

"Pete, that was years ago. That was before Mexico. That was before I knew how to have a relationship. I was scared. I was just a girl."

"And all that's changed?"

"Of course it's changed. I love you. I want to know what's happening."

"Oh Jesus," I said; suddenly the room felt small and hot. "I can't talk about this right now. I'm sorry. I'm sorry." I must have sounded shrill or desperate because she backed right off. "I need time to think. I need time to myself." This I just blurted out. I really hadn't even thought it before, and had she ignored or dismissed it, I might have never mentioned it again, but she didn't.

"Well," she said, "you have this canoe trip as soon as school's out. That's ten days of time to think."

"I need more. Maybe after that I'll go up to the cottage for a while." Although I wasn't looking at her, I felt her stiffen.

"How long is a while?"

"I don't know," I said with more annoyance in my voice than I wanted. "A few days, a few weeks." Then to myself but not to Lydia I said, "Give me the summer. Just give me until the end of the summer to figure things out." None of this had I planned or even thought about, but instantly it felt like the perfect, the only, the essential solution to a big problem I had only been vaguely aware of until a few minutes earlier.

"That's fine. Take all the time you need. Do whatever you need to." We both wanted very much for this conversation to be over, and now it was, and we didn't know what to do. "Well," said Lydia, "I'm going to make some tea. Want some tea?"

"I think I'll walk Art."

"You just walked him. You can smoke in here," she said. "Just sit by the window."

I opened the window and sat by it and blew smoke out of it. She busied herself in the kitchen, and there was the comforting clink and clatter of teacups and teakettle.

"By the way," she called to me, "did you take three hundred dollars out of our joint savings a couple of weeks ago?"

I rode my bike up the lakeshore into Highland Park against a north wind. It was cold and hard going, and I got a good workout, but coming back I sailed. Everyone was already crowded around a table in the oyster bar at Davis Street making funny, profane toasts to sloth, idleness, debauchery, dissipation, and two or three other vices.

"Chilly out there," someone commented.

"I should say. When's this damn weather going to break? I hate spring in Chicago." I got a pint of Guinness and raised it to Carolyn and Wendy, who were still in their work clothes but who were now wearing oversized T-shirts over their tailored suits. They were bright yellow and said EUROTRASH GIRLS across the fronts.

"So this is it?" I said. "Last day of work?"

"Last day until sometime in September," Carolyn said, clinking my glass.

"Last day forever," said Wendy, who claimed to have a plan that would allow her to never work another day in her life.

"What's your plan?" I asked.

She winked. Wendy and Carolyn are about as different as two friends can be, except that they are both smart. Wendy grew up a working-class kid in Berwyn, Illinois, and was the first member of her family to go to college; she had a brief, early marriage and is tough, brash, and aggressive in a way that has made her an outstanding, highly paid corporate attorney, who loves to drink beer, shoot pool, close bars, and who doesn't always go home alone. Carolyn is single, shy, subtle, thoughtful, discreet, stable. Each is what the other might secretly want to be, just a little bit.

"Where'd you get the shirts?" I asked.

"Officer Lotts."

Someone sang out, "Eurotrash girls," and we toasted.

Lydia knocked on the window from the sidewalk, then hurried in. Having come from the train, she, too, wore work clothes. She hugged me from behind with one arm and kissed me on the cheek as if Tuesday night had not happened. She got a glass of white wine and crowded into the table. She seemed confident and natural in ways I did not feel. I watched her with our friends as they talked and drank and laughed. She looked so happy. They looked so happy.

Someone else said, "So tell us about this trip."

"Oh, jeez," said Wendy. There was a villa in Aix-en-Provence that a couple she knew from law school was renting for the month of June. They'd start out there. There was a week of hiking in the Swiss Alps with some other friends. "You met the Thumas, didn't you?" Wendy asked me.

"Sure," I said.

Then they were going to Prague, then "into Hungary to look for Wendy's lost identity," said Carolyn. After that they planned a week of R and R on the Amalfi coast in a small hotel they'd read about somewhere, then on to the Greek islands.

"God, I'd love to be going with you," said Lydia, and I knew that she meant it.

"Why don't you, then?" asked Wendy. "Why don't you guys come join us in Switzerland for a week. You ever been to Lauterbrunnen?" Wendy described a narrow mountain valley with a flat, lush floor and sheer two thousand–foot walls over which one stream after another stepped into space, creating a dozen little waterfalls and rainbows everywhere you looked.

Lydia turned to me.

Wendy talked about taking cogwheel trains and cable cars up into the mountains in the mornings, hiking all day in pastures filled with wildflowers and cows wearing cowbells, surrounded all the time by snowcapped peaks, then taking your shoes off and sitting in beer gardens afterward.

"Write a couple of your pieces about it. Cover some of your expenses," urged Carolyn.

"This isn't just the wine speaking?" Lydia wanted to know.

"Of course not," said Wendy. She told us to book into the

Hotel Oberland and get a front room, so our windows, complete with window boxes full of red geraniums, would swing open right on the Jungfrau and the Eiger. "Big, soft quilt to sleep under. Downstairs in the restaurant they have a fish tank full of trout. You point out the one you want, and ten minutes later they bring it to you grilled."

"Sounds wonderful," I said. "When are you going to be there?"

"We meet Dick and Martha on the veranda of the Oberland for lunch on June 17."

"I can't do it," I said. "Maybe Lydia can—"

"Why can't you?" asked Wendy.

"Oh, I'm chaperoning a wilderness canoe thing up in Canada with a group from school; I'll be gone."

"Get someone to take your place," said Steve.

"Too late. Besides, I told the *Trib* I'd do a piece on it."

"On a bunch of teenagers on a canoe trip?" asked someone. "Who'd want to read about that?"

"Well," I said, "I was going to leave the kids out. Just write a kind of me-and-nature thing."

"He thinks," said Lydia, "that high school boys wearing Ray-Bans and lighting farts around the campfire might detract from the Thoreauvian quality of the piece."

"Can you do that?" asked Wendy.

There followed a fairly heated debate on the decay of journalistic standards and whether or not travel and other soft-feature writers have the same moral obligation to truth and accuracy as those writing on the front and op-ed pages.

"God, I need a cigarette," I said finally. "Ask that guy with the mustache if I can bum a cigarette."

"Change the subject!" said Lydia. "He hasn't had a cigarette in two days."

"Okay," said Carolyn, "I need a dog sitter or a house sitter, or both. Anyone know of a reliable friend or relative who
wants a place to stay for the summer?"

She needed someone to take care of her old Australian
shepherd, Cooper, while she was gone, but her ads had been
answered almost exclusively by college-age boys who were
way too interested in being just two blocks from Wrigley
Field and who she imagined holding Cooper over the back
porch railing to pee and using her splintered Mission style
furniture to build late-night bonfires on the roof deck.

Wendy was now trying to convince Lydia that we should
join them in France.

"I really can't," I interrupted.

"Why not?"

"He's got to solve the crime of the century," said Lydia.

There was a pause. Then Officer Lotts said, "This doesn't
have to do with that Korean chick, does it?"

"Not exactly."

"Oh Jesus Christ," said Steve.

"But kind of?" asked someone.

"Kind of, I guess."

"Oh Christ. Pete, you know what?" said Steve. "You're going a little nutty on us here. I think you need to talk to someone. That's what I'd do if I went a little nutty; I'd get right in
there and talk to someone." He left the table suddenly. There
was an awkward pause in the conversation.

"It's even part of my plan," Wendy said into the vacuum.
"How do you think I got the moxie to quit my job? I went to

a counselor." Together they'd decided Wendy was unhappy because she needed some time off. So that was Wendy's plan: quit her job, go to Europe, spend all her money, sue her counselor for malpractice, settle out of court, then open a chain of McDonald's in Uruguay or Chile and get involved in local politics.

"Bravo!" someone said. We toasted justice and the American way, self-interest, Machiavelli, and abject amorality. Later I got into a conversation with Carolyn at the end of the table and asked her directly if she'd ever gone to a shrink.

She hesitated. "Yes, when my father died."

"Did it help?"

"It did."

Much later I pushed my bike home and Lydia walked beside me. We were both quiet much of the way. Finally Lydia said, "I'm sorry I said that about the crime of the century."

"Okay."

We were quiet again until she said, "I want you to do me a favor. When you get back from Canada, I don't want you to go up to the cottage. If you need to do this thing, if you need some time, stay in Carolyn's place and take care of Cooper for her."

"What difference does it make where I stay?"

It somehow did. "Carolyn's is neutral ground. Stay there and help her out. Please. Will you do that for me?"

I told her that I'd already intended to go to the cottage for the weekend to grade papers. I did not much like Lydia telling me what to do with my freedom before I even had it, but I didn't like hurting her, either. I didn't like that at all. I told her I'd think about staying at Carolyn's, and, in an effort to change the subject, I said, "You know, you can go to Europe by yourself if you want to."

"Of course I can." As she bristled, I was reminded of two things: just how fiercely independent Lydia had once been, and just how much she had changed without my really noticing. It should be said, however, that neither her fierceness nor her independence had come naturally. Rather, they had been foisted upon her by careless parents who spent almost all their time fighting, complaining about each other, feeling sorry for themselves, and ignoring her. As a result she had become very tough and oddly territorial. Most of us are capable of being possessive about small spaces, duties, achievements, lovers, and sometimes friends. Lydia had been possessive about everything. She had divided the world quite clearly between hers and yours. Jack Purcell tennis shoes had been hers; I hadn't been allowed to own a pair. Glenn's Diner had been her restaurant. No matter how many times I ate there, I had always been an interloper. She had owned it. She had owned asparagus, Wedgwood blue, Virginia Woolf, the coast of Maine, all Woody Allen movies, the word "ennui," Auguste Renoir, and autumn, and she hadn't been very interested in sharing any of them. She hadn't been interested in sharing music at all, except Django Reinhardt. She had loved Jerry Jeff Walker until I had borrowed a CD, and she'd found it in my car one day. "What's this doing here?" she had asked.

"I've been listening to it," I'd said. "I like it."

She handed it to me. "Here. It's yours." As far as I know,

she never listened to it again. Now it seemed that she cared much less about "her things." Either that or I had become one of them.

Why had I answered so quickly that I couldn't go to Europe? I had the time; I had the money. I guess I didn't want to go; I wanted to stay home and get to the bottom of this Lisa Kim thing. Or maybe I didn't want to go with Lydia, not just when I had won some breathing space. Or maybe it was some of all of that. And if I really wanted to find out about Lisa Kim, why had I signed on for the canoe trip? But I knew the answer to that one. I'd done so at a time when I was spending half my days running after Lisa Kim, and half running away from her, thinking that if I ran fast and far enough, my life might get back to normal. It happened on a day when I was running away from her. I said yes, and just to seal it before I changed my mind, I pitched my idea for an article to the *Trib* travel people, and they said yes, and so I was committed. Good. Now I wasn't so sure.

I called Carolyn the next day and told her I'd take care of Cooper if she couldn't find anyone else to, but I didn't mention staying in her condo. I also asked more about the counselor she had seen, and finally, if she would mind giving me his name. "No," she said, although I wasn't so sure. Was she territorial, too? "Gene Brooke; he's in the book."

Gene and I sat in a narrow, tall, bright room on living-room furniture. Gene was a slender, balding man with a goatee, an earring, and an easy manner. Before he could ask me a question, I asked him one. I wanted to know if people can ever really change, if they can make fundamental changes in themselves. I was thinking of Lydia, but I suppose I knew I was also thinking about myself. Gene looked at me thoughtfully, and I wasn't sure he was going to answer, but then he did. I would find in the weeks ahead that he often did the unexpected, that just when I was positive I knew what he would do, or he as psychologist would do, he'd surprise me. "I believe that they can and sometimes have to. Not often—once, twice in a lifetime at most. Never easily, because real change is wrenching. But sometimes people have to find a new path, go a different way. I couldn't be in this line of work if I didn't believe that. Now, can I ask you a question?"

"Sure."

"Are you uncomfortable being here?"

"Sort of."

"Can you tell me why?"

"Well, I don't know. I guess I feel that coming here is kind of an admission of failure," I said.

"How so?"

"Well," I stalled. I looked at him trying to decide if I was ready to confide in him. It was the fact that he had answered my question that allowed me to take the chance. I told him that growing up I'd been a worrier, that I'd worried about everything, but that I'd learned to quit worrying. It had happened that year when Lydia and I had lived in Mexico. I could almost say it happened one Sunday afternoon when I was out exploring the farms and villages in my car and the oil-pressure light on my dashboard came on. At first I panicked. I was fifty miles from anywhere and thought I was screwed. The car was the only thing of value I had. Then, as I sat there by the side of the road looking at the little red light, I began to have a conversation with myself. I said, "What's the worst that can happen? Your car's shot. Suppose it is. Suppose you leave it here and never see it again. You walk away. You walk to a paved highway. You sit down in the shade and wait for a bus; Mexico is full of buses. It takes you to another bus or to a town. Tomorrow you're in Mexico City. The next day Chicago, if you want to be. In ten years you won't remember how much the car was worth. You'll laugh about it. It won't even make a very good story. It's okay. You can handle this. In fact, there isn't anything you can't handle.' That became my mantra, and it stood me in good stead for a long time. In a tight spot I'd just step back and say, 'There isn't anything I can't handle.' It worked. It has worked until recently."

"And what happened recently?" Gene asked.

"It stopped working. I've run into something I don't seem to be able to handle."

"And it has shaken you."

"It's shaken me badly." I told him about my anxiety and irritability. I told him I felt alone, isolated, panicky, unable to concentrate, unable to work, sometimes claustrophobic, sometimes afraid that I would lose control. "I've depended on this thing, and now it's gone."

"Do you think it's gone completely?"

"Seems to be."

"I kind of doubt it," he said. "My guess is that you've just found out that you have limits. We all have them, and maybe you've discovered yours." He told me that finding and then accepting personal limits was one of the last stages in the maturation process. Another was knowing how and when to seek help because most of the time most of us can handle most things, but not quite always. He asked me if I could modify my mantra.

"How do you mean?" I asked.

"Well, can you add a word or two? Can you live with 'There's almost nothing I can't handle'?"

"Maybe."

"'And then I know where to get some help.'"

"Here?" I asked.

He said yes. He said he would help me sort through things if I wanted him to. I thought I did.

"Why don't you begin by telling me about what you're having a hard time handling." I told him about Lydia and me; then I told him about Lisa Kim. I told him everything, even about the wet dream. When I finished, I felt self-conscious. Later I would think that he did not. Later I would come to feel that Gene Brooke was the least self-conscious person I knew. "So anyway," I said, "so anyway." I chuckled. "My friends are concerned about me. They think I'm going crazy. They think I'm obsessed. I don't know; maybe I am."

He looked at me thoughtfully. Again he spoke when I didn't expect him to. "I don't think you're crazy, and 'obsessed' is probably too strong a word. I think you're preoccupied. I think there's something deep inside you that's eating at you." He said he could help me look for that thing, and we made an appointment for the following week. At the door, he asked me what happened with my car.

"The car? Oh. Nothing. It turned out to be nothing. I drove the car another couple years and sold it."

———

I was relieved. Gene Brooke had treated me as if I were normal, and it reminded me of how many people were not doing that just then. I got Art, bought a *Trib* and an *Evanston Review,* and sat on the sidewalk at Café Express. The sunshine on my face felt very good. I read the seven-day forecast and made some short-term plans for the first time in a while: haircut, ball game, library for some audiotapes to listen to in the car. I read all the sports stuff including the Cubs minor-league statistics. I checked out the Ravinia schedule and read a movie review. I looked at the police blotter and obituaries. Then there they were: the Doctors Kim. Looking out at me from some hospital benefit side by side smiling in black tie and pearls. Jesus. I mean, true, the North Shore is not that large a place, but really. I turned the page and read a review of a new Japanese restaurant, then turned back. Was there something of Lisa's smile on her mother's face? Was there any hint of their tragedy in their eyes, the slope of their shoulders? They were not alone in the photograph. A woman at the table behind them was laughing, pretending not to see the camera. A slim, handsome man who actually did not see the camera was rising from the table, turning. A waiter was leaning to place something on the table; you couldn't see what.

I turned on but then turned back again. There was something about that photograph. I carefully tore it from the paper, folded it, and put it in my breast pocket. I licked the suds and drained my latte and tried to think of something else to do so I wouldn't have to go home.

John Thompson came into my classroom after school, and sprawled in the chair across the table, his hands clasped behind his head as if neither of us had any finals to grade. He was as straight as his name, a big, crew-cut, poetry-spouting, Shakespeare-quoting, Marine of a man with whom I had started at Lake Forest, and against whom I had competed for a couple years when our enrollment was shrinking and there were fewer and fewer positions. We both managed to survive and made a connection in the process that grew into a friendship when he got divorced and I listened to him about that for a couple of years, and continued undamaged when he recently became department chair and my boss.

"Let me see that picture again of the girl who was in the accident," he said.

"Why?"

"Just let me take a look."

I dug the obituary out of the drawer and handed it to him. He studied it. "I think I saw her in a mattress commercial."

"You're kidding."

"No. Bunch of adults jumping on mattresses like kids. Some mattress-outlet store. She was funny."

"Funny? I don't think of her as funny." And I was reminded once again how very little I really knew about Lisa Kim.

"She was pretty funny." He tossed the article on the table.

"I'll look for it," I said.

"I hear you're going on the canoe trip," he said.

"Yep."

"You got a lot of work?"

"A shitload." I hoped he'd take my curtness as a signal, but he didn't. He had a purpose.

"Listen," he said, "we've had some calls about the papers you haven't returned. Jay wanted me to speak to you."

"I know. I'm going to Michigan to grade all weekend. I'll mail them out Monday. You don't have to worry about it." The 'Jay' part was to let me know the administration was in the loop.

" 'I' am going to Michigan, not 'we'? Something going on?"

"Maybe. I'm not sure yet."

"Are you okay?" he asked.

"Not really, but it's nothing a summer won't cure."

"You want to talk?"

"I don't know what to talk about yet. I may when I do."

"Well," he said, "I've wondered from time to time. It always has been a marriage of convenience, and there's only so much weight those can bear. Has something happened?"

"Not to me, but maybe to her. She says she's gotten closer to me, and I guess I haven't gotten closer to her."

"Closer?" he said a little dubiously.

"Listen, she's like she is because she was hurt badly when she was younger." My explanation sounded canned even to me; perhaps I had offered it too often. Was I defending her again? I had long been aware that not all of my friends liked or valued Lydia as I did. John was one of these. He found her aloof. Well, she *was* aloof. She had a habit of both making and breaking friendships with great ease. I saw it many times. Someone new would come into our lives and for a period of time be given a leading role, and then—just that quickly—be dismissed. It was as if Lydia needed to prove to herself that she could have real relationships and then prove that she could do without them. John Thompson among others saw this as insincerity on Lydia's part; I saw it as another self-protective device. And again I was aware of how different things were now, how much Lydia seemed not to want to do without me.

It was a cool, breezy weekend and I set up shop on a card table in front of the fire in the cottage. I read, graded, wrote, read, graded, wrote, read, graded, wrote until I just couldn't anymore, and then I chopped wood or raked leaves for a while. I grilled some pork chops and ate them with brussels sprouts and wild rice. I also thought a lot about Lydia's request that I stay at Carolyn's. I had pretty much decided not to honor it until Sunday afternoon, when Art and I went for a walk on the beach. To my surprise, we found Carolyn sitting on the bench in the corner of her deck reading a novel; I took her presence there as an omen. She didn't look up until I came up the steps.

"Hey, Pete. Hey, Art." She let Cooper out, and he and Art went down the stairs to feint and gambol on the sand. We watched them and talked. Wendy was already in France. Carolyn had wanted a week to decompress after working fifteen-hour days for weeks to close out her job. She'd been here alone reading and sitting in the sun, and I saw now that her hair was bleached white blond and that her freckles were all out; her face and arms were brown against her bright white sweater. She said, "I'm glad you came by; I was going to call you today about bringing Cooper over. I'm leaving Tuesday." She squinted into the sun and smiled the kind of smile that makes you feel that life might not be so bad after all. "Move

out of the sun," she said. "Come sit." She put her book down
and pulled her knees up to her chest. She was barefoot despite the coolness.

"Are you alone?" I asked.

"Yep."

"No little architect?"

"No little architect," she laughed, but didn't elaborate.

"So, what are you reading now?" We talked about books
and authors. She told me about the plot of her novel.

"Would you still like someone to stay in your place?" I
asked.

She looked at me uncertainly.

"I mean me. That way Cooper could stay in his own house."

"You? Just you?"

I nodded. She cocked her head. "What's going on?"

I shook my head.

"Well," she said, "I'd have to know that it's okay with
Lydia."

I told her that it was Lydia's idea and that she'd volun-
teered to keep both dogs while I was on the canoe trip.

"Well," she said, and I could see that she was worried
about getting in the middle of something, "that would be
great, I guess, if you really want to; I'd want to phone Lydia
and talk to her." We made tentative plans to meet in the city
the next night so that she could show me the fuse box, give me
keys, go over Cooper's routine. When we finished, the ease of
conversation we had had earlier was gone. I said something
about getting back to work and left. On the beach, I threw
a stick for Art. He and Cooper both went after it. I looked
back. Carolyn was still sitting, still reading.

I got up at four on Monday morning. In the breast pocket of the flannel shirt I slipped on against the morning chill, I found the newspaper photo of Lisa Kim's parents and the camera-conscious woman laughing and the oblivious man rising; there was something in the picture that made me want to look at it and look at it some more, so I taped it to the mirror in my bathroom at the cottage and studied it as I scraped three days of stubble from my face. Then I forgot it. I left it there. I had locked up, carried my shopping bags down to the car, and driven into the city before I realized it. Just as well. I probably would have had an accident gazing at the damned thing.

I avoided stopping by the apartment. It was still cool, so Art could sleep all day in the car. He didn't mind that at all. I called Lydia from school and was relieved when she didn't answer. I tried to sound casual on her voice mail. I told her I'd run into Carolyn and made all the arrangements. "She leaves tomorrow, so I guess I'll stay over there tomorrow night." After I hung up, I tried to tell myself it was no big deal.

I decided I wouldn't tell Gene Brooke about the whole business with Lydia. It wasn't out of any desire to obfuscate, but out of a need to get on with the Lisa Kim stuff. It turned out that he wasn't in as big a hurry as I was, but it didn't matter anyway, because as soon as I sat down, I told him everything. I thought I was getting it out of the way, but he didn't; he thought I was introducing it. It was his belief that Lydia and Lisa probably weren't two separate issues, that it probably wasn't coincidental that they were happening at the same time, that I probably needed to understand my feelings for

Lydia before I dealt with Lisa Kim. All of this seemed terribly obvious when he said it, and I felt foolish or naïve for not having seen it. Jesus, my feelings for Lydia? Why had I not stopped to examine these more thoughtfully? I guessed that I was sad. I guessed that I felt some relief or release, but also some guilt; more than anything, I was pissed off.

"Can you tell me why?" he asked.

"Because she's acting as if this whole Lisa Kim thing is some kind of frivolous lark, and she's treating me as if I'm Don Quixote, off tilting at windmills."

I thought he might ask me if I *were* tilting at windmills; if the tables had been turned, I probably would have asked him, but Gene seemed seldom to ask the next question, the obvious one. I wondered if not doing so was a technique, something he had studied and learned. I imagined grad students sitting on folding chairs in a circle asking each other unexpected questions. The one he asked me was, "What do you think that Lydia feels?"

Lydia? Jesus. I didn't know. It was as if I were going on a journey, and he was asking me the most basic questions: Have you packed a bag? Have you purchased a ticket? Have you planned your itinerary? I'd done none of it. I guessed that Lydia, too, was angry. I guessed that she was hurt and worried. I guessed that she was resentful.

"Why do you think she feels those things?"

"Because she's possessive."

"Which is something you had both agreed never to be, so you're angry."

"Exactly," I said.

"But why is she possessive?" he asked.

"I don't know."

"Is she afraid of losing you?"

"Maybe."

"Why is that do you think?"

"I don't know."

"Could it be because she loves you?"

"I guess."

"Okay," he said, "would I be twisting your words too much if I said that you are mad at Lydia because she loves you?"

I had to think about that for a while. "I suppose not. We weren't supposed to fall in love with each other."

"So she's violated your agreement?" Then he wanted to know why Lydia would have ever agreed to such a thing in the first place. Why would she want to be in a relationship not based on love? We decided the only reason would be if she was afraid of love. And if she was no longer afraid of love, wasn't that good? Didn't it say that she was healthier and more mature? And why had I ever wanted to be with someone who was neither of these things? Was I, too, afraid of love?

I needed time to think. "I was different," I finally said. "I doubted the existence of love because I didn't think I'd ever really been in love."

"And are you now?"

"No, but I think I can be. That's the difference. I think Lisa Kim's death shook me by the shoulders. It said, 'Look, that could be *you* crumpled there.'"

"So you've changed, too, like Lydia," Gene said.

I had to admit that I had. Then why was I mad at Lydia

for changing? Was I mad at her because I didn't love her? Was I mad because she wasn't lovable enough? Suddenly our time was up, but I didn't want to stop. Gene insisted.

"Man," I said, "this is hard." We agreed to meet again before I left for Canada.

Speaking the truth to Gene made me feel like an honest—if foolish—man, and seemed to ease my anxiety a bit. I wanted to do more of it; on Saturday I went to see Tanya Kim. She was fitting someone, so I waited and looked over the boots on display. She noticed me when she came out with arms of shoeboxes: "Oh, hi."

"Sell me some stuff for a canoe trip?" I asked.

While I waited, I picked out a waterproof poncho, a flashlight, a pocketknife, and an unbreakable water bottle.

When Tanya came, she looked at these things. She recommended a different knife and two pairs of water shoes. "You don't want to cut your foot out there," she said. Then she sold me some socks and T-shirts that breathe and dry quickly, and a pair of nylon fishing pants with zip-off legs.

While she was ringing me up, I asked her how she was doing. I again made my question general, but she again answered in the specific and with the same air of confidentiality I'd felt from her before. I decided I'd reciprocate and told her about going to see Gene Brooke. This interested her. She said that her father had wanted Lisa to see a counselor and was now after her to.

"I don't suppose Lisa ever did . . ."

"Of course she did."

"Really? That surprises me a little," I said.

"Why? It was the perfect Lisa situation. Someone else agrees to sit still and listen to you talk about yourself for a whole hour. You must not have known her as well as you thought you did."

Did I detect that she was tempting me to tell her the truth? I decided to meet her halfway. "Tanya, I didn't know her at all. That's another reason I came in here today. I wanted to tell you that I wasn't Lisa's boyfriend."

She cocked her head and maybe she even smiled a little bit. "I'd kind of figured that out."

"Do you know who I am?" I asked.

"No." She had finished bagging my things, and she was looking into my eyes now, maybe for the first time.

I took a little breath. "I saw the accident. I was right behind her. I was the first one to get to her. That's my only connection to her." I watched her closely; she seemed okay. She then carefully asked me the obvious questions: How did it happen? Did she say anything? Was she conscious? Was she even alive?

Finally she handed me my bags. "I got your letter," she said. "Have you talked to Rosie Belcher? She was Lisa's best friend. If anyone can help you, she can."

"Yeah, I made the connection in the yearbook, but I just can't find her. She's not in any directory, and neither are her parents."

"They moved to the East Coast after Rosalie got married, but she's still around here. It's Rosalie Svigos, now. She's a doctor." Some small thing had changed. She met my eyes again. She listened when I told her about my trip. She said she hoped I would have a good time.

Gene had me go through the accident again, looking for the thing that was bothering me. We went minute by minute. He asked me lots of questions: How would you have approached Lisa? What if she'd locked her door? What would you say to her? Are your emergency flashers on? Does she have bucket seats? If you take her key, doesn't her steering wheel lock? He asked me over and over to imagine the best-case scenario, to imagine everything going right.

"Well," I said, "I guess she probably wouldn't say 'thank you very much. I know I'm drunk as a skunk, and I really appreciate your saving my life.'"

"Okay, but suppose she does. Suppose she cooperates and doesn't scream or Mace you or shoot you. What next?"

We went through the whole thing; there were a thousand problems. "But Gene, I've known that. I've really known that all along, but there's still something bothering me. It's like the name of a state capital or movie director that's circling my head, and I can't quite reach out and grasp it." I asked him if there was a memory drug that might bring the thing back. He didn't know of one. He said that we could try hypnosis, that he used it sometimes to help people quit smoking or lose weight or deal with anxiety.

"And it works?"

"Sometimes. It depends on the person. In your case, I think maybe we're looking in the wrong place and it might help us find the right place. Have you ever heard of George

Mallory and Andrew Irvine?" He told me about the two British mountain climbers who disappeared on Mount Everest
in 1924. No trace of them had ever been found. In the meantime, Sir Edmund Hillary and Tenzing Norgay climbed Everest, followed by dozens of others, and every one of them had
the same goal: the summit at 29,000 feet. Every one. Then,
a few years ago, a young German climber named Jochen
Hemmleb shifted his sights ever so slightly, and said that he
wanted to climb to 28,000 feet, not 29,000, and he wanted to
reach Mallory and Irvine, not the summit. So he calculated
the most likely place where the climbers would have fallen,
went right there, and found Mallory, who was actually in one
piece, preserved by the thin, cold air, including his clothing and
equipment. Then Hemmleb found dozens of other climbers, although not Irvine, in the same bizarre graveyard of a
boulder field in various states of preservation, many identifi-
able by nationality and expedition because of the clothing
they were wearing and the equipment they were carrying.
So now orthodontists from Dallas and socialites from Marin
County and whole Japanese climbing clubs have gotten to
the top of Everest, but Jochen Hemmleb went somewhere
entirely different and found something entirely different because he changed the angle of his quest by a fraction of a
degree. "So maybe that's what we need to do," said Gene.

"Explain how hypnosis fits in," I said.

Gene asked me to think of my mind as a circle with a
horizontal diameter. Above the line is the conscious mind
and below it the unconscious. Apparently hypnosis, which
is really nothing more than a relaxation technique, can allow

some people to sink a bit below the line, a bit into their un-conscious, where they may discover the forgotten or the re-pressed and where suggestion can sometimes be planted.

I told Gene I thought I might be a bit too much of a skep-tic or cynic to be a very good subject, but I'd think about it.

"Is the Gene Brooke in your story the same one who works at this school?" asks the dog-faced boy.

"Yes," I say.

"Then how does he know Carolyn O'Connor? Did he used to work in the city?"

"Actually, he doesn't know Carolyn O'Connor, or didn't then, and he's never worked in the city. I just rearranged the pieces a little for the sake of the story."

"I don't understand," says Nick.

"Well, it just works better that way," I say.

"I'm not sure I agree," says the girl whose hair is blue today, "and I definitely don't buy this hypnotism stuff. That sounds hokey to me. Sounds like Seinfeld or something."

"But that's the part that's true," I say. "Gene really *does* use hypnotism and he really *did* use it on me."

"Now let's see," says Nick. "You put something in that isn't true because it works better, and you put something in that doesn't work because it's true. I'm not sure you can have it both ways."

"Sure I can; it's my story," I say.

"Isn't it *my* story, too?" asks Nick.

"You as the reader? Well, yes," I say.

"What if I don't buy it?" asks Nick.

"Do you buy it?" I say.

"I'm not sure," says Nick.

"So Gene Brooke is our Gene Brooke, and Carolyn O'Connor's real, too?" asks the girl with blue hair.

"Yes."

"And you say they know each other when they really don't?"

"Well, they didn't. They do now," I say.

"I'm confused," says the blue-haired girl.

"And you can make that happen just because it's your story?" asks someone.

"Yes."

"Okay," says the dog-faced boy, "if the story belongs to the writer, and I'm the writer, then why can't I write anything I want to just like you? Why do I have to write this stupid double-plot story?"

"Is that a rhetorical question?" I ask.

"No. I'd really like to know."

"I'll give you a serious answer if you really want one."

"I do."

"For one thing, the double-plot story forces you to be aware of the narrative voice, forces you to think about the relationship between the narrator and the other characters for another, and it helps in story development, helps your story to be dynamic and not static. A lot of times beginning writers have trouble making a story happen. This assignment forces you to make things happen," I say.

"I don't want to be forced, I just want to write. Can't you just let us alone to write?" says the blue-haired girl.

"Well, that would be a bit like teaching you to swim by pushing you into the water. My job is to show you a few strokes."

"But this is supposed to be 'creative' writing," says Nick. "That suggests freedom to me. It's more like 'restrictive' writing when we have to do your assignments all the time."

"Then make up your own assignments."

"Can we do that?"

"Sure. I'd prefer that you do that. The more responsibility you take for the course, the more you'll get out of it. But your assignments have to be as good as mine, and I have to approve them. Write them out. Use mine as models, if you wish. Make sure that each one has a specific stated goal or goals and a specific purpose, and the purpose cannot be to exorcise your adolescent angst or explore formless, amorphous, and misguided teenage impressions of love, lust, or any related topic. Sorry. I mean goals and purposes that have to do with the craft of writing, the technical discipline of writing."

"Can I ask another question? If this is a writing course, why are we doing all this reading?"

"Well, you know, writers read other writers just like golfers look at each others' swings and young surgeons learn from old surgeons, and artists study under other artists. It's kind of how you learn."

"Learn what, though?" asks Nick. "To imitate other writers? What if you want to be completely original?"

"Well, most people would say that it's impossible to be completely original, that all work is derived from what came before it. That's the current word: derivative. Everything is derivative, nothing is original."

"I refuse to believe that," says Nick.

"Well, of course you do, and you should. You're eighteen years old. You're inventing the world as you go. Other people would say you're *re*inventing the world. Later you may agree with them, or you may not. It's like sex. Every generation thinks it invents sex and all the words that go with it. It's difficult to think of your parents doing those things—"

"Please."

"—or using those words, but they obviously did. Every generation is pretty sure it invents all the dirty words, but they are some of the oldest words in any language."

"Okay," says Nick, "what's your story derived from?"

"Mine?"

"The girl who got killed in the car."

"Well, I don't know. I really hadn't thought of it."

"Aha! The principle applies to everyone but you, then."

"No. It applies to me. I just hadn't thought of it. It's not a conscious thing."

"Don't you think your story's completely original?" asks Nick.

"What do you mean?"

"I mean mixing fact and fiction like you do, moving the pieces around, sort of blurring the line between what's true and what isn't."

"Well, I may think my story's original," I say, "but it probably is not."

"Isn't that pretty important?" asks the dog-faced boy.

"What?"

"That it's probably not original."

I say, "I think it's more important that I think it is."

"Then you're saying illusion is more important than reality," says Nick.

"What I'm saying is that very often illusion is all we have."

8

• • •

TRAVEL WRITING

DATELINE: QUETICO, ONTARIO, CANADA
by Pete Ferry

The real importance of the [Quetico-Superior wilderness canoe country] lies in the values we find there and that we take with us when we leave, although we may not quite understand them.

—Sigurd Olson

I MET TOM MAURY at the Candlelight for some beers and asked him about Quetico. "The mosquitoes are as big as hummingbirds," he said, "the water's as cold as Dick Cheney's smile, and it's the one thing I've ever done that wasn't overrated."

Quetico Provincial Park is 1,500 square miles of carefully regulated, damn-near-pristine wilderness territory in southwestern Ontario adjoining Minnesota's equally extensive Superior National Forest. It is an uninhabited tract of water, woods, and granite in which the only travel allowed is by canoe. At that, permits must be arranged weeks in advance to discourage casual or frivolous visitors. No cans or bottles are allowed in the park and everything else that is packed in must also be packed out. The name itself may be an old Chippewa word, or it may be an acronym for the Quebec Timber Company, which once held leases in the area. Whatever it once was, it is today one of the least-spoiled, most-assiduously-guarded preserves on the continent. It is the land of sky-blue waters.

Our outfitter's base camp was a mile and a half across Cedar Lake by canoe, I suppose just to give us the flavor of the thing. We zigzagged there on a warm June evening.

We ate ham and beans in a dining hall that took me back to the Boy Scout camp of my childhood. Then there was talk of what to do and what not to do. Hang food bags eight to ten feet up out on a limb. Don't swim without tennis shoes; a cut toe can be a serious problem in the wilderness. Don't leave any fire unattended, even briefly.

Our guide was not a wizened, pipe-smoking Finn as half-anticipated. Rather, he was a nineteen-year-old named Mike from Bosnia by way of Romeoville, Illinois. His parents fled the war at home, and although he was given to braggadocio and double negatives, I decided to trust him on the assumption that he knew something of survival.

We took a swim test after dinner, and I plunged right off the pier, hoping, I suppose, to prove my mettle or some such thing. The icy water literally took my breath away, and I dog-paddled twenty yards gasping and choking.

Then we each learned how to hoist the remarkably light (70 pounds) canoe onto our shoulders. We packed and re-

packed our knapsacks, each time designating a few more ne-
cessities as frills to be left behind. And, finally, we crowded
around a picnic table and studied maps by gaslight. There
was much route tracing and wonderful guide-talk about
This Man and That Man Lakes, Poobah Creek, the Wawiag
River, the Bitch and the Bastard, Chatterton Falls, and Have
a Smoke Portage.

Day One, June 6:

I was awakened at 5:00 by the soft gray dawn, mosquitoes
in my ears, and rain on the roof. I lay there for half an hour
thinking about cigarettes. I had been smoking twenty of
them a day on and off for almost twenty years. Now I had
five Merit Ultra Lights that I bummed in a moment of panic
to last me nine full days.

I covered myself with insect repellent and wandered out.
It was drizzling. I interrupted a girl kneeling with a towel
across her bare shoulders at the lakeside, trying to wash her
hair.

I found a seat in the dining hall, read a story by Kathryn
Shonk about feeling far from home in Russia that seemed
eerily prescient, and impulsively smoked all five Merits before the others arrived for breakfast. Cold turkey.

There were seven of us in the three canoes (I was the only
smoker) with provisions to last nine days. Among us we carried nine large backpacks, seven life preservers, and seven
paddles. All of these things had to be transported by hand
when we portaged, or traveled overland from one body of
water to another.

Three of the packs contained all of our personal things,

from clothing to flashlights to sleeping bags. One held a nine-by-twelve–foot canvas tent that, in turn, held all of us. Five packs contained food and cooking items. They were labeled breakfast, lunch, supper, staples, and bread. Included were seven fresh steaks, seven bratwursts, two pounds of bacon, some smoked sausage, some processed cheese, peanut butter and jelly and, of course, bread. Then there were the dehydrated foods ranging from Chicken Tetrazzini and Beef Flavored (?) Stew to Apple Brown Betty.

The first half of the day we paddled toward Canada, most of us spending more time in a canoe by noon than we had in all our lives. We went along quietly for the most part; the little adventure we had planned looked somewhat foreboding from this vantage point. In my head I was humming the old Eagles tune "Take It Easy"; I always thought the line about the women ("four that wanna own me, two that wanna stone me, one says she's a friend of mine") was really a fairly transparent bit of braggadocio, but for the moment I was very happy to be in a canoe heading to Canada away from two women who had been making my life complicated. One of these I once drove several miles out of my way to call from a phone booth "standing on a corner in Winslow, Arizona," but that was a long time ago.

At the border there was a picturesque little waterfall, a tiny customs office, and a ranger station right out of *Yogi Bear* that was manned by the businesslike but grandparently Mr. and Mrs. Mike O'Brien. I wondered if there was another international checkpoint in the world where the only traffic was canoes. (Waiting for our papers to be processed, I bought a cigarette from a teenage girl. I felt quite criminal.)

Mike had been complaining all morning about the motor-boats that are allowed on the American side of the border. "Maniacs," he called their drivers contemptuously as they hummed by. I imagined that he was trying to impress us with his Sierra Clubbishness, but after gliding a few miles north, he had us stop our paddles and listen. We could hear a tiny brook that looked to be half a mile or more away. We could hear the voices of two people in a canoe just approaching the brook. We could nearly distinguish their words.

Our first campsite was just as I had imagined it. There was a clearing, a small, thick meadow. There was a wood of birch, cedar, and spruce, the rocky bank of a clear, cold lake, and even enough sun for a sunset.

We ate our tough little steaks and hash browns from metal plates as we stood around the fire. Coffee was brewing over the flames. I felt for my smokes.

Day Two, June 7:

The land of Quetico is primordial. Geologically, it is nearly infant. The last ice age ended a mere 10,000 years ago. During it, huge glaciers some two miles thick ground and ground at the earth until there was nothing left but its skeleton of stone.

Then life began anew. The melting ice supplied the end-less lakes and waterways, but the land lay skinned. Even now, the soil is so thin that it is often impossible to dig a hole of more than four or five inches. But remarkably, from this frag-ile epidermis has grown one of the world's great forests.

As a kid, what impressed me about Manhattan was not the size or distinctiveness of its skyscrapers, but the number of them. So it was in the North Woods. From the middle of

Lake Agnes, I could see thousands, hundreds of thousands, perhaps millions of trees. They were all I could see. They stretched several miles behind me, several before me, and half a continent beyond me.

We had our first real portage. It was across a long, steep trail littered with boulders that ranged in size from bowling balls to suitcases. It was exhausting and discouraging. How many of these lay ahead?

But then we crossed placid Lake Agnes to Louisa Falls, where the waters fell thirty feet into a swirling caldron and then forty feet more. We stripped, plunged in, washed our hair in the foam, got very clean, ate cheese and salami sandwiches on the pine-needle forest floor beside the water and even the mosquitoes left us alone. (The Quetico skeeter is legendary and a local joke was that it's the provincial bird. Portaging with a canoe over your head, you sometimes had to hold your breath to keep from inhaling the infernal bugs.)

Hale and renewed, we paddled hard up Agnes with the sun on our backs. We stopped early, camped on a pretty island across from hundred-foot bluffs, dried our clothes on the rocks, fished, climbed the bluffs, sunbathed. Just as the travelogue said.

By quirk of circumstance, there was not a watch among the seven of us. In the past two days, I had never known the exact time. There was some sense of liberation about this, but it was unsettling, too.

Day Three, June 8:

Physically this was perhaps the worst day of my life. We were off early under low, fast clouds. A strong wind at our back moved us quickly, but churned Agnes as well. Where we crossed her, she was nearly a mile wide and running with whitecaps. I was frightened, but we made it without mishap.

We then leapfrogged from one back lake to the next, trying to reach a special rookery and fishing ground. We crossed seven portages in all, the last especially long and rugged.

By now it was raining. We headed for our last portage, one of more than a mile, but were driven back even on this small lake by the wind and slashing rain. Mike said we had better wait out the rain at the first campsite we had seen in hours, but the rain came harder and colder and didn't let up. We crouched pointlessly behind rocks and finally struggled to put up the tent. Those of us who had dry clothes put them on, and we all got into our sleeping bags. It was late afternoon, and the tent swayed and sagged with the water and the wind. We were all asleep within minutes.

I am a city boy at heart. I like baseball parks and public transportation. As a rule, I take my nature in small doses such as postcards and summer cottages. This dose was clearly too large.

I awoke and it was the same gray light it had been all day. My dreams had been phantasmagoric and my mind raced. I distrusted my vision, but there were no straight lines in the tent against which to test it. I wanted very much to know the time. I imagined myself at home with one of the two women I mentioned earlier, entertaining our friends. We were serving roast chicken, wild rice, and fresh asparagus; there was white wine on the table and good music in the air. But I wasn't at home. I was in the opposite place. I was a grown man approaching middle age who was desperately, painfully homesick.

I wrote this the very next day, but already that night had all run together in my mind. There was a jolly period, I remembered, when the rain lightened, and we told dirty jokes and even sang a song. Then there was more heavy rain, and we realized that we wouldn't have a hot dinner. The tent began to leak. The rain dripped, seeped, ran in rivulets, stood in puddles.

Mike said that food in the tent might attract bears, and we knew that there would be no dinner. He told us to press together for warmth. Our soggy bags squished as we did so. We were seven men in the middle of Canada lying back to belly like spoons. We dozed, started, twisted, and shivered all night long.

Several people had spoken the word "hypothermia." I had come along on this trip because it was free, I was free, and I thought I might get a story out of it. I had no idea that it could ever become dangerous.

Day Four, June 9:

Dawn, and it was still raining. Then, shortly afterward, it stopped. Three of us raised our heads and looked at each other. We crawled out into the wet gloom.

We huddled to assess our situation. We had not seen any other people since the previous morning. We had crossed seldom-used portages to a remote lake in search of walleye. We faced a mile-long portage through a swamp and an all-day paddle before there was any chance of meeting other campers. And, if it rained, they would be able to do little for us, anyway.

We studied the sky. It looked as if it would rain again any

moment. The least-wet things we had were thoroughly damp. Everything else was sopping. We had to dry out. We had to build a fire. We had to eat. We had to try to dry some clothes.

We all whittled away at wet branches until we had created a small heap of dry tinder. We skinned twigs and raised a smolder, a flame. It was an hour before the fire was truly established. It had not begun to rain.

On a graph, the day was an upward parabola from there. We cooked up eggs with bacon bits and hash brown potatoes. We built a bonfire after breakfast and rigged up clotheslines hither and yon, threw sleeping bags across bushes and tree limbs, dangled wet socks from canoe paddles, roasted tennis shoes, heated rocks and put them in the tent to dry it out. And all day long we moved back and forth deeper and deeper into the woods dragging logs and fallen trees, sawing them, breaking them, building our woodpile.

Our fire roared. A mist rolled in and left. It did not rain. That thing that happens to people in common need had happened. With each dry piece of clothing folded and put away, our spirits rose. We joked freely now. Someone got together a softball game with a pair of rolled, wet socks. We made popcorn and hot chocolate and stood around the fire eating, feeling our drying pants and socks, telling stories.

After one task or another, I reached for a cigarette. It had been three days, and I had had little problem. No swollen extremities, raw nerves, or temper tantrums. But I expected to smoke. I expected to with coffee, after food, when I wrote. Because I simply couldn't, I did not miss it terribly. But had I been able to, there were many times I would have without hesitation.

Later there was even time to fish and canoe to some nearby Indian pictographs. We read and wrote by the fire. Someone shouted in celebration of a patch of blue sky. We ate a huge, hearty, awful dinner of turkey supreme, green beans, and pineapple cheesecake. The west was pink. I predicted the next day would be wonderful.

Day Five, June 10:

Through the wet early days, we said many times, "At least it isn't cold." The next morning it was raining, and it was cold.

It was easy now to understand why people who live outside have often worshiped nature. At home if it rained, I closed the door and turned on the tube. Here, so much depended on the weather that was rolling across the sky. Everything. If only because there was no place to escape it. It may seem silly since it was nearly summer, but the question of survival had already arisen. It did again this day.

We packed up and ate a cold, quick breakfast in near silence. Then we paddled away. Our long portage was difficult, sometimes through muck that was waist deep. It took most of the morning. The long paddle that followed was just as hard. The temperature was around fifty, and we were all wet. Lake Kahshahpiwi was choppy, and it continued to rain.

We were looking for an abandoned fire watchtower high on the hills above. Mike claimed that he did not know there was an abandoned ranger station there as well, but in retrospect, I was not so sure.

Anyway, we rounded a bend and someone said, "A house!" We all repeated the word. It was a little white cottage. It had been four days since we had seen a house, a car, any sign of civilization but those we carried; anything but water, trees, and rocks.

Mike approached tentatively, read something on the door, turned the handle, and went in, was back in a second, shouting, "Come on up!" We cheered and suddenly we were very cold. We could barely grip the packs to carry them. Inside we struggled awkwardly with knots and buttons.

There were three rooms, and right in the middle, a wood-burning stove. Soon we had a fire blazing and clothes drying. We cooked up chicken-noodle soup and a huge batch of grilled-cheese sandwiches.

The sign on the door read, "Please replace what you use with something else. Leave the place clean." It had many reciprocating messages: "Saved from the rain. Dorth of the North," "Replenished wood supply. Thanks, The Wassons," and, incongruously, *"Où est le boeuf?"*

The rain stopped. By late afternoon there was a line of blue across the northwest. Then slowly the clouds were rolled away above us like the lid of a sardine tin, and it was lovely again. Mike, I thought, felt a little guilty about staying over here. The rest of us enjoyed it thoroughly. I tried not to think what we would have done had this place not come around the bend.

We had made our long detour in search of fish, but it was here that we found them. We were out in the canoes and on the little dock until well after dark. One of us caught a twenty-two–inch lake trout.

Day Six, June 11:

The day we had been waiting for. We were up early and were instantly busy like the Seven Dwarves whistling, cooking, sweeping, cleaning, sawing, and drying. We replenished the cottage's wood box and its larder with macaroni and cheese, dehydrated fruit, and some encouraging words.

Each of us polished off four pieces of French toast and syrup, and then we were off into this cool morning of pure, bright colors. I am a practical person. I do not consider bill-boards the ultimate proof of society's decadence, nor moderate air pollution a threat to my life. I am willing to put up with some of the trade-offs that modern times demand. I think that people who care more about baby seals and sperm whales than other people are just a little warped. And if the wilderness is sacred to me, it is so in the lower case. After all, none of us will ever really live in it again unless all of us do, and I know that we would not want that. Quetico is a laboratory. Still, I should note that in six days, I had not seen one discarded can or gum wrapper, one cigarette butt, one old matchbook, used condom, or pop-top. And when the sun shined, you had to blink your eyes because so much beauty seemed impossible. And the whole country smelled like Christmas.

We traveled all day through half a dozen lakes, across nine portages. It never got hot, but the sun was warm. Finally there were the McIntyre Falls, sharp, bubbling cascades, and the long, winding McIntyre River, beaver territory with one dam after another. We walked our canoes down it in sometimes-chest-deep water, just like Bogart in *The African Queen,* and if the setting wasn't as exotic, the mosquitoes were certainly as big.

But by evening, the sky had clouded. It began to rain as we fixed dinner, and we went to bed feeling fairly defeated, despite the day.

Day Seven, June 12:

Rain again. It had rained each day. We found it tiresome and oppressive, but I would have thought it impossible. It was not. It was only uncomfortable.

Like most people, I make fun of weather forecasters. It was only in the absence of their prognostications that I realized how much attention I paid to them. There were times this week when a good forecast would have given us much-needed hope, and a bad one would have crushed us.

In addition to weather forecasts, we had now spent a full week without each of these for almost the first time in our lives: any broadcast, any recorded message, a newspaper, a phone call, a shower, any electrical appliance except for flashlights and cameras, a toilet, a mirror, a letter, a roof (save one), and a spigot. Around midday we passed two fishermen and paused to exchange a few words. They were the first people other than ourselves whom we had seen in over four days.

We had become fairly competent paddlers. Today we glided single file and in near silence down the wooded, grassy Tuck River hoping to surprise a moose. There was a great crash in the bush that may have been one, but no one saw it. Nonetheless, we felt proud and serious about our quest.

Evenings had become our best times. Most had been clear and peaceful. Tonight we camped above Basswood Falls, the prototype for rapids everywhere. We swam and washed, ate more mush and pretty good lemon pie, watching the clouds lighten and finally flee. There was a seagull nesting on a rock just out in our lake, and one of us went off to photograph it. Two other canoes drifted about on the still water carrying solitary readers and writers. Others of us fished up and down the rapids. And all of us watched the huge moon coming up and adding its bright yellow reflection to the deepening colors of the dusk. If it were always like this, I would never go home.

Day Eight, June 13:

Some time after midnight, I'll be damned if there wasn't a violent thunderstorm. There was suddenly so much water in the tent that we almost needed snorkels. It was evidence of our fatigue and resignation that no one even bothered to get up. When the lightning passed, we went back to sleep in puddles.

I had been intending to write a cute little piece about all the wildlife I had *not* seen on this trip, but today ruined it. Coming down Pipestone Bay, we spotted two black-bear cubs on the shore. Then just beside us there was a loud confrontation between a giant seagull and a bald eagle. Interestingly, the seagull was the aggressor with many swoops, dives, and squawks. In truth we had seen half a dozen eagles, though none as close. And we had seen various hawks, many elegant and dignified blue herons, and always the loon, which seemed so much more at home beneath the water than above it, and whose self-pitying warble is Quetico's sound track.

Again we had a long paddle on a cold gray day, and again the sky cleared late in the afternoon. Our campsite was beside Pipestone Falls in thick woods. We made blueberry pancakes and laid our bags and ourselves out on the grass to dry. A couple of us fell sound asleep.

Later I crossed the bay to walk beside the rapids. I turned

a corner and was close enough to a beautiful big doe to touch her. I started, she bolted. But moments later I saw her again and froze. She was fifty feet away, and when she saw me, she came as close as thirty feet. She pawed the ground as a bull might and even feinted in my direction once or twice. Perhaps she had a fawn nearby. This lasted half a minute, and then she was gone noiselessly into the heavy bush.

I had seen, touched, even hand-fed many deer in zoos and parks, but it was thrilling to meet one where it was at home, and I was not.

Day Nine, June 14:

We came back to base camp, to beds, saunas, and late-night glasses of Drambuie with new friends, people who do the remarkable routinely. Someone offered me a cigarette and, at least for the moment, I didn't want it.

Sometime that summer some other men-children and I would make our annual visit to Great America to ride the roller coasters. We would dare and tempt each other. We would keep track of the rides we went on as if they were accomplishments. We would pretend that the danger was not illusionary, that there were not backup systems on backup systems, that someone's finger was not always on the stop button.

I realized now that the only reason we paddled off three days from anything was to find a place where we couldn't dial 911, signal time-out, or cry uncle, where the only backup systems were within ourselves. Back in the city, several people would ask, "Did you have a good time?" They did not know—as I did not know before—that the question was ir-relevant. In fact, I think I asked it of Tom Maury not so many weeks ago. And now I understood his answer: "It's the only thing I've ever done that wasn't overrated."

The last day paddling home, the sky was clear, and the sun was warm. There was no threat of rain.

9

• • •

FINDING PETER

IN A CHILI'S IN DULUTH, squeezed into a booth with a bunch of fart-joke-telling, elbow-wielding teenagers, I ate a rib-eye steak, mashed potatoes, and a Caesar salad, and I drank a tall, cold Weissbier with a slice of lemon. This was one of the three or four best meals of my life. It was, in fact, so good that it seemed to demand a cigarette afterward, and I stood for a long time looking at packs of them in a convenience store before not buying any.

I got back on the bus, reclined my seat, and slept through the rest of Minnesota and a good bit of Wisconsin. When I woke up, there was a videotaped movie on the monitor above my head. I watched it drowsily; it was shot in Chicago. A car pulled up and the driver talked to a man on a bicycle. The shot was over the bicyclist's shoulder framing the driver's face in the open window. Lisa Kim was sitting in the passenger seat. She said, "We're going to be late." Good God. For the first time, I felt that I couldn't escape this woman even if I wanted to. Later there was an interior shot. Two girls were talking in the foreground, and Lisa Kim was sitting on the couch painting her toenails in the background. She leaned over one raised knee to do it. She seemed oblivious to the conversation and to the camera. I watched the credits at the end of the movie: Third roommate—Lisa Kim.

Out in the wildernesss, I had thought a good bit about Lisa Kim's death and my own; it's an easy thing to do when you are two or three days' paddle from a phone and another half day from an emergency room.

I looked out the bus window and thought about the Mallory and Irvine story Gene had told me. I liked it. I enjoy subtle lessons in direction and misdirection; sailing west to go east, the kid who looked at the ground while everyone else was looking at the sky. But if we were looking in the wrong place, where in the world could the right place be? Perhaps this wasn't about Lisa Kim at all; perhaps it had nothing to do with her. Maybe it was about Lydia and me and how we may have wasted our lives waiting for something that might never happen. Or had happened and wasn't much to write home about. It was difficult to believe that this person who had been the human being I felt closest to for most of twelve years might one day stop speaking to me, at least in an unguarded way, might never whisper in my ear or laugh spontaneously at something I said. Or maybe it was all about me: early-onset midlife crisis. There had been times in the last year or two when I could not make my job *not* boring. Or maybe it was about my father's death; I *had* been thinking about him a lot. Or maybe Lisa Kim was like a grain of something that gets in your eye and scratches it, and feels like it's still there, so that you think you have to rub it long after it's been teared away or flushed out.

"How are things with Lydia?" asked Gene.

"I haven't talked to her."

"Why not?"

I told him that when I went by to pick up the dogs, she wasn't there, and I was relieved. I was no longer as angry, but I thought I might be feeling guilty.

"Is guilt a feeling you've had often before?"

"Sure. I believe in guilt. I think it's good in small doses. Reminds me of the consequences of the stupid things I do."

"Tell me about one of the stupid things you've done. Tell me about one you've felt guilty about for a long time."

I told him about a kid who showed up on the beach one summer whom we called Joe Cavalier. He was nerdy, but we treated him like he was the most popular kid around. It was a conspiracy, and I knew it was wrong, but I was a sheep. I went along with it. And then one day he figured it out, and he went in his aunt's cottage and didn't come out again the whole rest of the summer. I'd always felt bad about that.

I told him about a quiet girl who had a crush on me. She asked me to dance out of the blue and then pressed against me real hard. I took her under the bleachers and felt her up. She let me. She wanted me to. Afterward I lied and said I had to go home right away because I didn't know what to do with her, or maybe I was embarrassed to be seen with her when they turned the lights on. Later I was with a bunch of guys on a street corner, and she went by in her father's car. I'd always remembered the look on her face.

"Did you ever apologize to her?" he asked.

"No, I never said anything."

"Are you still feeling guilty about Lisa Kim?"

I told Gene that what I was feeling was more like anxiety. It was more like there was something I still had to do, but I didn't know what it was. When I woke up in the morning, I knew right away that I had to do it. I'd be in the middle of something, completely absorbed, and I'd know suddenly that there was something I had to do. It was like a dream in which you know you're supposed to be somewhere or do something, take a test or do something important, and you just can't get there and do it. You're missing a class, and the semester's going by day after day; you know you have to go, and you can't. You never do. You always remember too late. You never get there, and you just keep getting in deeper and deeper shit. "It's like that," I said, "but in this case I don't know what it is I'm supposed to do. Can anxiety drive you crazy?"

"Well, anxiety can be a foundation for some compulsions. And so can guilt." Gene smiled at me as if he were admitting something. "Which is why we've been talking about guilt."

"Do I have a compulsion?"

"You are compelled, but I don't think you're exhibiting enough symptoms to qualify as a full-blown case of OCD. Sorry." He smiled again. "And yet something is still bothering you, something that we haven't been able to uncover." We both smiled. I was beginning to feel that we were regular smiling fools that day.

"Do you still think hypnosis might help us find this thing?" I asked.

"I don't know. It could."

I had expected to have time to myself on the canoe trip, but of course I didn't; when you are in real wilderness, you huddle together for safety and warmth. If you do go away for a moment's solitude, you hurry right back. Where I finally found myself alone was, not surprisingly, in the middle of the city, in Carolyn's bright, airy condo that occupied the top floor of a brownstone three-flat. It had skylights, a big bed, a comfortable couch, and a little back deck with flowerpots on which I sat in the mornings with the dogs to read the paper or write and sometimes in the evenings to think, drink a beer, listen to the crowd noises, and look at the lights from Wrigley Field two blocks away. Her home became a place where I didn't feel anxious, where I made all the rules and decisions, and I made good ones. I didn't eat out of cans over the sink, I did my dishes before going to bed, at least at first, and I never got very drunk. I planned meals, grilled lots of chicken and fish, used Tidy Bowl and bed linens, and when I got lonely I called someone, but never after nine.

I'd never really lived alone, except on the road. Some years before I'd begun traveling alone sometimes simply because I'd get assignments or opportunities when Lydia or my other friends weren't free. I dreaded the first of these trips, but was pleasantly surprised to discover that I enjoyed my own company. Now I have a whole catalog of memories that I share with no one: bullfights, public baths in Budapest, riding a bike along the Danube River or beside the North Sea in

Zeeland, a particularly tasty meal of ginger crab and Tiger beer in an open-air restaurant on a rickety pier at the end of a Star Ferry run in Hong Kong. The truth is, if you want to write anything, you can't mind being alone, and I was writing a lot. I was writing the story of Lisa Kim that I had started in the spring. I was just getting caught up to the moment, and I was about to have a lot more to write.

"I want you to hold out your arm in front of you," Gene said. "Make a circle with your thumb and index finger. Now I want you to relax. Your arm is going to begin to tire. You can probably feel it tiring already, feel it getting heavier. As it does, let it slowly sink toward your lap. Getting tired. When it touches your lap, then you'll be completely relaxed. You'll be very, very relaxed. You'll be aware of your own breathing. Feel your breathing. Your arm's getting more and more tired. It's heavier and heavier. It's sinking. Your eyes are closing. There. Now, as I ask you questions, it may be that your subconscious will remember something that your conscious doesn't. If that happens, if that were to happen, your right index finger will rise, will go up. And if that happens, then I'll try to help you go back and find out what your subconscious wants you to know. Okay?"

"Okay."

"Let's try something a little different," he said. "Let's begin with the accident and work backward. See if we uncover anything backing up."

"From the moment she hits the lamppost?" I asked.

"Yes. Start there. We can always go forward if we need to."

"I'm watching. It seems as if I'm watching from back at

the light, but I couldn't be. It's too far, and people would have been honking, so I'm driving; but she whizzes out in front of me; she hits the curb on the right once, I think, and doesn't even attempt to turn into the curve, doesn't even try. Maybe she is passed out already. Who knows."

"What did you say?"

"When she hit the lamppost? I think I said, 'Oh sweet Jesus! Oh my God!' I pulled into someone's driveway and put on my flashers. I started to run to the house, but someone had already opened the door. I yelled to call the police."

"Let's work backward."

"From the light? Okay. I'm watching her. I know she's in trouble. I never decide what to do. It's not as if I had decided, and then she pulled away, and I was too late; I hadn't decided. But before we get to the light, I'm hoping for the chance. I'm hoping that we both have to stop, and then I'll be able to do something, but we're half a block away when the light turns red, so we have to slow down, we have to stop, and it's a short light, anyway. There just isn't time."

"Go back," he said.

"I'm following her; she's easy to keep track of because she has a broken taillight. I'm following at a distance because I'm afraid she'll veer into oncoming traffic and someone will swerve and hit me. I'm desperately looking for a cop. I'm thinking, 'how do I signal a cop if he's coming toward me?'"

"What are you feeling?"

"Fear. Butterflies."

"When do you start feeling afraid?"

"When she hits the curb. She just bounces off the curb, and I know she's fucked up."

"What are you feeling before that?"

"Annoyance, I guess. She's driving fast and recklessly, and it pisses me off. First she's behind me following too closely, changing lanes, so I slow down, pull over, let her pass, but then she hits that curb . . ."

"When are you first aware of her?"

"She has her brights on in my mirror—"

"Go back before that."

"Let's see," I said. "I'm not . . . I don't know. I don't remember before that."

"Okay. That's okay. Just keep going back until you do remember something."

"Well, let's see. That would probably be all the way back to school."

"Okay, go there. What time is it?"

"It's almost six. It's quarter to six. I can see the clock on my classroom wall. I'm late."

"What are you late for?"

"We're supposed to go out to dinner with Lydia's boss, Don, and I'm cutting it close. I'm trying to grade one last paper, and I just can't concentrate on it. I finally get it done and look up. It's quarter to six. I remember our date. I say, 'Oh, shit.' I call home and leave a message. 'Sorry. Change the time if you can.' I put all the papers I have to grade in my briefcase. I lock the room. I get into my car. It's dark. It's cold. Not real cold, but damp cold. It's rained some. The streets are wet. I'm not sure beyond that."

"Do you make any stops?"

"Actually, I do. I'm on Green Bay. I pull into Sunset Foods in Highland Park. I buy a bottle of wine because I'm late.

Jacob's Creek Cabernet. I buy something else. Tums. Oh yeah, I've got acid. I've been burping all afternoon. Terry in the cafeteria made ham salad, so I have it for lunch with a bowl of split-pea soup. Too rich. I'm burping. Then about five, I impulsively eat the sandwich I'd brought for lunch. Now I'm really burping, and I'm mad at myself. I'm not hungry, I have a tension headache, I'm late and I have to go out with Don, who has two beers and starts telling bad wife jokes in front of his wife. God. Traffic's bad. Oh Jesus. I almost have an accident. That's right."

"What happens?"

"I'm still on Green Bay, but in Glencoe now. I'm trying to open the Tums with one hand, you know, work my thumbnail between two tablets through the paper. I look down for a nanosecond and almost hit the stopped car in front of me. I hit my brakes, honk, the guy behind me hits his, almost slides into me. I hold my breath. Pull around her. Then—"

"Your finger's up," Gene said.

"What?"

"You've raised your finger."

"Really?" We both look at my finger.

"Go back to the almost accident. Describe it again." I do. "Okay, what kind of car was it?"

"It's raining. It's dark."

"Try."

I tilt my head back against the chair. My eyes are as heavy as ball bearings. I let them sink toward the middle of my head. "Small. Black. Japanese. The right taillight is out." We sit a long time. It is quiet in Gene's room. "It's Lisa Kim," I said.

"Are you sure?"

"Well, it's either her or an identical car. *Her* taillight is out, too."

"Do you know that when you were describing the accident, you said, 'I pulled around her'?"

"I did?"

"Why is the car stopped? Are you at a light?"

"No. We're right in the middle of a stretch of road," I said. "Someone's getting out, I think."

"Is it Lisa Kim?"

"No. The other door, other side."

"Can you see who it is?"

"Not very well. It's dark. It's rainy."

"If you had to say, is it a man or a woman?"

"If I had to say, I'd say a man."

"Tall or short?"

"Taller than shorter."

"Fat or thin?"

"Thinner."

"Older or younger?"

"I don't have a read on age, but there's something—"

"What?"

"I don't know. There's something recognizable about the person."

"Dark or fair?"

"Hard to say. Dark, I think."

"Can you get an emotional read?"

"How do you mean?"

"How would you describe this parting?" Gene asked. "Is

it amicable? Did she slam on the brakes and order him out? Does he lean over to say good-bye?"

"Hurried is all. He must have heard me screech my brakes. It's like 'Gotta go. See ya.'"

"Where's he go?" he asked.

"Don't know. I have no sense of that."

"Do you see the black car in your rearview mirror once you pass it?"

"I don't think so."

"Go back to Sunset Foods and come back down Green Bay. Could you have been aware of the car before you nearly hit it?"

"I don't think so."

"How about after you pass it? What then?"

"Well, I have one of those talks you have with yourself sometimes. I say, 'Listen, asshole, what the hell is wrong with you? It's Christmastime. It's Friday night. You're going out to dinner, secretly you like Don's bad jokes, and you just missed having an accident, so lighten up, for God's sake.'"

"And do you?"

"I do. I cut over to Sheridan Road in Hubbard Woods even though it's a little slower and take the scenic route. I switch from NPR to Christmas music. I start singing Christmas carols. And I'm still doing that when she comes up behind me with her brights on."

"Back to the car you almost hit, did you see the face of the person who got out?" he asked.

"Not really."

"Hear his voice?"

"No, no. I don't know what it is . . . something . . . something . . ."

"You're tired, aren't you?"

"Yes."

"Let's stop for now. Keep your eyes closed."

"Okay."

"I'm going to count from ten to zero. With each number, you'll emerge a bit more from hypnosis until we get to zero. Okay?"

"Okay."

Afterward, we just sat there for quite a while. I *was* tired. I closed my eyes again for a long moment, and when I opened them, Gene was smiling at me. "You found it," he said. "You found the pebble in your shoe. I was pretty sure it was there."

"Were you?"

"Yeah. You don't seem nuts enough to be nuts."

"How very clinical."

"You like that?"

"I do." We talked about why I hadn't made the connection before. Gene thought that I'd been traumatized by the accident and maybe even suffered mild shock. He didn't think it surprising. "What you saw was momentous," he said. "What happened before it was insignificant by comparison. I imagine you just forgot it. Your conscious mind filled up with the facts and the feelings of the accident, and there wasn't room for anything else. Also, there was some time between the two incidents and, maybe more important, some changes. You changed routes; you changed moods. Maybe you just didn't connect the two cars."

"Now that I have, what can I do about it?" I asked.

"I'm not sure. Maybe nothing. I'd sit on it a day or two and see if your anxiety level goes down. If it does, then maybe you've done enough just to make the connection."

"If it doesn't?"

"If I were you, I'd wait a while. I think you'll know what to do when the time is right."

As it happened, my anxiety level did not decrease. In fact, it increased, but it was not the same, dull, troubled, aimless nervousness I'd felt before. Now it was keen and focused. Who was the guy in the car? What was he doing there? Why did he get out? Why did he allow Lisa Kim to drive away to her death? And what was there about him that was faintly familiar? I sat around for the two days Gene recommended and then picked up the telephone. If I was going to answer my questions, I'd have to learn more about Lisa Kim. Tanya had said that Rosalie Belcher Svigos was Lisa's best friend, so I called her at the Chicago hospital where she was doing her residency.

At first it didn't seem as if I would learn much from Dr. Rosalie Svigos. She didn't shake my hand or let me buy her a blueberry muffin or decaf coffee in the hospital cafeteria. In fact she was so cool, I wasn't sure why she'd agreed to meet me at all, yet she had. She was a big, pretty woman with such a don't-bullshit-me quality about her that I had to remind myself that she was only a year older than Lisa. She sat there in the noisy cafeteria and watched me suspiciously as I fairly babbled. But she *did* sit and watch me even though I was telling her hardly anything; I was dissembling although I hadn't intended to—there was something in her demeanor that made the whole last-guy-to-see-her-alive story sound fanciful and unlikely.

She interrupted me in mid-sentence. She asked who I was. A reporter? An investigator? "Did Lisa's father hire you? Or was it the insurance company?" Confronted, I told her the whole improbable tale, and I could tell she found it improbable. I could also tell that she wasn't about to give up anything on her friend, that she was there to protect Lisa. But from whom? A bumbling high school English teacher with a bad conscience? Still, she sat, and there had to be a reason for that especially after she found out I was no threat to Lisa, but when I asked for information, she gave me the party line: Lisa was a brilliant actor. Like any true artist, she challenged people, made them think about the line between reality and illusion, the nature of artifice, everything they believed. She was an intuitive actor who was always practicing her craft. She was a minimalist who never appeared to be acting. She was a genius who had little time for fools, who didn't mind being misunderstood or making enemies.

"Did that cause problems with her career?" I asked.

"What do you mean?"

"Is that why they dropped her from *Gangbusters* before they took it to New York?"

"They begged her to go to New York," Rosalie said. "*She* was the one who said no."

"Why in the world would she do that? Wasn't it, like, her big break?"

"Big breaks only matter if you are looking for one. She was looking for a character. When *Gangbusters* opened in the back of a bar on Lincoln Avenue, she had a minor role. In the next two years, they rewrote the whole thing around Lucy Fantisimo. She became the lead. Her character took over the play. That was all Lisa. By the time they were ready to go to New York, the thing had been compromised to death, bastardized. One thing about Lisa, she was not a compromiser. She was an absolutist. She said no. She was bored with the part. She'd given everything to and gotten everything out of *Gangbusters* that she could. She'd moved on."

"Pardon me, but moved on to what? Waiting tables?"

"Let me tell you something," Rosalie bristled. "Lisa Kim could find more dramatic possibilities in a four-hour shift than some actors find in a career. But no, she was not just waiting tables. She did an experimental film that was remarkable, she did an Off-Off-play that was interesting, and she wrote a play that Bruce Kaplan is thinking of producing in the spring. Plus, she'd been cast in a big-time independent film called *Dream Car* that was shot in New York last spring. I think it's going to be huge. I think Lisa was about to get a lot of recognition."

Unlike many doctors I've known who are well trained but poorly educated, Rosalie Svigos had ideas, and I knew that I'd found someone who could help me. But now she'd said her piece, and she was looking at her watch. I needed to act quickly. I said, "A few minutes before the accident, I saw a man get out of Lisa's car. Do you know who that might have been?"

Now she was looking at me again, and sharply. "What did he look like?" she asked.

"It was dark. My impression of him was that he was tall, thin, and dark haired."

"Where was this?"

"On Green Bay Road in Glencoe."

"Glencoe?" she said to herself.

I took another shot. "At the time of the accident, Lisa was high on heroin."

"My God," she said, "where'd you get that?"

"There was a private autopsy."

"Do you know what heroin does to you? It makes you nod. It makes the world go away. It makes you feel nothing. That was the last thing in the world that Lisa Kim would have wanted. She wanted to feel everything. She was the most alive person I ever met. Now if you told me cocaine—something that would heighten sensation—I might believe you, but . . . Lisa did not use heroin."

Rosalie got up to go. I couldn't think of a way to keep her. To my surprise, she fished a business card out of the pocket of her lab coat and put it on the table. "If you find out who the man in the car was, I'd like to know." She hesitated, then spoke again. "You don't find heroin in an autopsy," she said. "You find opiates—the stuff heroin comes from—but morphine comes from it, too, and codeine that's in some cough medicines and in Tylenol 3. She could have taken Tylenol 3 for a toothache and tested positive or eaten a poppy-seed bagel. Lisa was not using heroin."

I could have run Lydia over the next day, and not even seen her. I know I had things on my mind, but I should have seen her, anyway. It happened like this: I was driving and thinking. I knew that I knew something about the man who got out of Lisa Kim's car that night, but I did not know what it was. Something. Could I have met him? Could I have recognized him? I turned off the radio and let my mind drain. I was driving. I needed to move in order to think. I had called Lydia to ask if I could come by for some things. It was time that we had some contact anyway, although actually I had hoped she wouldn't be home; I thought the call might be enough. Besides, I was really just looking for an excuse to be in motion.

Lydia was just leaving for a run, and I wondered momentarily if her stretching exercises against her car, her expensive New Balance running shoes and her Lycra outfit were meant for me. I had always been the one who exercised, and she had often teased me about being vain. We exchanged a few self-consciously pleasant words like neighbors meeting in the supermarket; then she took off and I went upstairs. I poked around. I had forgotten what I had come for. I was thinking of that night, trying to re-create it once again as I had with Gene, but this time, slow it down one more click. I wanted to capture a detail I had so far missed. Some detail. Any detail.

Absently I stacked some books and CDs, then put them in a plastic bag. In my mind I was back in the school. I was locking my classroom. What exactly did I say to Thompson? I realized that I was closing a door right now, but it was the apartment door. I realized that I was in a parallel situation at the moment; I was going down a flight of stairs. I was getting into my car. Perhaps I could physically re-create what happened. Did I turn on the radio immediately? Did I leave it off? I pulled through the alley and stopped at the next street. I sat there idling; what had I been wrestling with that night?

Something. What in the world could it have been? I had my foot on the brake; I checked my rearview mirror. Remember. Remember. What had it been? Now there was someone in front of my car. Someone was bobbing up and down. She slapped my hood with the palm of her hand. "Hey!" she yelled. It was Lydia. She was running in place. I hadn't even seen her; how long had she been there? She came to my window. "You okay?"

"Yeah."

"What are you doing? I couldn't get your attention."

"I was thinking. I was just thinking."

She slapped the hood again, waved, and ran off. I watched her go. I hadn't seen her there. She'd been right in front of me, and I hadn't seen her. I remembered then that there had been a time in my life when all I wanted to do was look at her.

When Lydia had gone away that time early on for three and a half weeks with another guy, I hadn't missed her at first, and then I had, and then I had terribly. I lay awake in bed wondering who she was fucking and how and when (right now?) and where; I imagined it was a wry, long-legged copywriter with tousled hair she'd once introduced me to at a party. I tried not to call her at her office, and when I finally did, our conversation was brief; she was busy, distracted, dismissive, self-protective in her "none of your damn business" mode. When she had finally come home, weary and wistful, I was in love with her, or thought I was. At the very least, I wanted her in a way that I had not before someone else wanted her. It was the strongest feeling that I'd ever had for a woman, and so I called it love, and perhaps it was. I needed to remember that.

I went back to Carolyn's place and lay on my back on the floor with my palms to the ground. My anxiety, which seemed to bloom full after any contact with Lydia, was manifesting itself in two ways: as something akin to vertigo and as a form of agoraphobia. I was scared of my own height; I felt too tall and conspicuous, though I am not very tall. I wanted to be shorter, lower, smaller, flatter. I also wanted to be alone. In crowded places I felt panic. Grocery stores with their fluorescent lights were particularly bad. One day I left a full grocery cart in the middle of an aisle and fled. The noise in restaurants sometimes got inside my head. Twice I'd had to make lame excuses and go out to my car to lie down across the backseat for a while. Sometimes I held onto the table or chair with both hands. I was afraid that I might just slowly topple over or slide under the table. Another antidote to all this madness was movement. Like a shark, if I kept moving, I could feed and breathe and stay just ahead of my demons.

For a couple of days after seeing Lydia, I avoided human contact, slept on the floor, and rode my bike. Gene told me to wait, so I waited. The first day was muggy and misty, and I rode slowly north along the lakeshore, picked up the North Shore bike path in Lake Forest heading west, turned north on the Des Plaines River bike path, and ended up in Libertyville at an old barroom called The Firkin that has good food and great beers on tap. I ate a salmon sandwich, drank two cold glasses of Hoegarden and read some of Eric Hanson's *Motoring with Mohammed*. When I started back, the sun had burned the mist away, so I found a bright, grassy spot beside the river, intertwined my legs with my bike, and slept on my back for an hour before riding back to the city. Then

I sat on the deck with Art, Cooper, and my book, and read until dark.

The second day I rode the lakeshore south to Hyde Park. A front had passed through in the night, and the pavement and grass were wet with the showers it had brought; the air was cool and clear. I stopped often to look at the city and the lake, to watch boats coming and going, a basketball game, the dogs at the dog beach, and the black, Puerto Rican, and Vietnamese fishermen along the rocks and harbors. I spent an hour in the 57th Street Bookstore, and bought Jochen Hemmleb's *Ghosts of Everest* about the search for Mallory and Irvine, bought a falafel and a big iced tea on 55th Street, and rode down to the lake to eat. That evening I took some cold beers and sat outside at Penny's Noodles to eat Thai food and finish reading the Hanson book.

The third day I had a phone message from my mother, who had moved to the cottage for the summer. She said that there had been a rain and the gutters had overflowed; they needed cleaning. Could I take a day or two to come up, clean them out, and spend a little time? I was happy to do so. She is a reader and napper who was unlikely to intrude on my solitude. Besides, I'd been wanting to take a ride on the Kal-Haven bike trail that runs on an old railway right of way along the Black River. I put my bike and Cooper in the back of my station wagon and Art in the front, where he leaned against the door and looked out the window like a teenager. I listened to an audiotape of Joyce's "The Dead," and I thought how pure an example it is of Keats's line, "Beauty is truth, truth beauty." Sad truth. The sad truth good men have to face about themselves. "Would I?" I wondered. "Have I? Am

I even a good man?" I listened to the last paragraph again. It was training, I thought, for writing Molly Bloom's monologue. I love the way Joyce turns words back on themselves: Snow "was falling on every part of the dark central plain, on the treeless hills, *falling softly* upon the Bog of Allen and, farther westward, *softly falling* into the dark mutinous Shannon waves."

In 1900 it took a day to get to southern Michigan from Chicago by steamer. In 1924, when my grandfather first made the trip, it took eight hours by car, and then you often had to walk over the last few dunes carrying your bags so the cars could climb them without getting stuck. Today it's two hours from the Loop by superhighway, but then, when I'm falling asleep at night on our porch, I can hear the trucks on that highway and sometimes I can see the lights of the nuclear-power plant across the dunes to the north of us and even hear the steam rising from the cooling towers. You can get there easier today, but it's not quite as far away. Life is as full of reversals as Joyce's syntax, I thought to myself. Once the world was wild except for pockets of civilization. Now the world is crisscrossed by highways, contrails, and microwaves, except for a few preserved pockets of wilderness like Quetico. Going there is fabricated adventure, postmodern and artificial just like the adventurers of today, rich people who climb mountains and sail balloons around the world unnecessarily. But if this old cottage in the woods was also an illusion, it was one I valued. I stood on the roof, my hands in wet work gloves, and I could see only woods and water all around and beneath me all the way to the horizon.

I like cleaning gutters because it is a dirty, easy job. The dirty part lets you feel accomplished. The easy part leaves time for the beach. I took my chair and umbrella there and read much of the afternoon. The water was cool and cleansing, and I shampooed my hair in it. Cooper lay panting in the wet sand, and Art played with a long stick, asking everyone who passed to throw it for him. My mother had made a beef stew with carrots and leeks and we ate it on the porch with French bread and red wine. I went to bed early listening to the calls of night birds.

When I got up at dawn, my face felt grubby, and I realized that I hadn't shaved in a while. I took a few minutes to do so, and there he was in the photograph of Lisa's parents clipped from the paper and still taped to the mirror. He was the other man; he was the man at their table. It was the way he was rising and turning simultaneously, just as he rose and turned, stepping out of Lisa's car that rainy, December night. It was the angle of his back, his posture, the way he held his head. It was he. "I'll be damned," I said out loud.

I did not run back into the city as I was inclined to do at first. I took my bike ride, although I admit to being distracted and now remember the trail as little more than a long green tunnel. It could not be a coincidence. He must have known them. He must have known her. Perhaps he was another doctor. If so, his apparent neglect or indifference was even more troubling. But could I be sure? Was I certain or was I desperate? I stopped my bike, straddled it, dug the photo out of my pocket, and unfolded it. I was certain. On some essential, visceral level, I was absolutely certain.

The next day was Saturday, so I packed up the dogs and my bike and headed back into the city in time to catch Tanya

Kim at Outfitters. "I want to see if you know someone." I handed her the photograph.

"Are you kidding?" she said. "Is this some kind of joke?"

"Not your parents. Him. That guy."

"Oh," she said. "No, I don't think so."

"I thought he might be a friend or maybe a colleague of your parents."

"I don't know him," she said.

10

• • •

THE SUMMER OF LISA KIM

A S I LOOK BACK NOW, it seems to me that the summers of my boyhood often had themes, although I don't know quite how they got them nor which one went with which year. It was all fantasy stuff, all self-invention. One summer a bunch of us spent weeks blazing trails through the Michigan woods. We trampled them, mapped them, and marked them by painting tin-can lids and nailing these to trees. Another summer a friend and I started a lawn-mowing business with an emphasis on the business part; we spent all the money we made on business cards, triplicate-receipt books, and clip-on ties. Another time a bunch of us formed a band, although no one could really play an instrument. We sat around someone's basement wearing yellow-, pink-, and blue-tinted sunglasses, pounding, beating, strumming and wailing really bad songs. We spoke of record contracts. A couple summers we played softball every morning from ten to noon and kept meticulous personal records; in the end we had almost as many at-bats as the big leaguers we were imagining ourselves to be. When I was a little older, I saved up my money and bought a secondhand drafting table, and one summer I was an architect wearing white short-sleeved shirts and designing a toolshed my father later built. The next summer, a friend and I wrote a daily comic strip about turtles because turtles were about all we could draw.

That summer I lived at Carolyn O'Connor's—the summer of Lisa Kim—I indulged myself as if I were a kid again. This time, of course, I was a detective. It wasn't all that hard to do, either, with ten weeks free and no one there to shake her head or roll her eyes. It involved imagination, prevarication, and a lot of telephone calls. The first of these I made to the hospital where the Kims were on staff, and the second to Miriam Prescott, the woman who was the head of the hospital's special-events committee. She invited me to meet her at her club.

In the Fitzgerald/Hemingway debate, I side with Hemingway and then some. It seems to me that money often insulates people and makes them silly, like the Kronberg-Muellers and their circle in Mexico. I thought Miriam Prescott would be like one of them or else a long-faced patrician woman in tweed, despite the heat. Instead she had buck teeth and freckles, and I felt bad about taking advantage of her almost before I knew that I was doing it.

I was surprised to be led to a café table on a terrace beside the tennis courts. "I took the liberty," she said as we shook hands.

A waitress was already delivering fancy tuna-salad sand-

wiches with elegant little homemade potato chips, cornich-
ons, big stuffed green olives, and glasses of iced tea.

"A working lunch," she said, pleased with herself. "I can
always justify it when the cause is good."

"Well," I said, "this is . . . thank you."

She waved me off. "Just like Henry to make all that fuss
and be so cross and then send someone right over. Anyway,
where shall we begin?" On the phone I'd told her that I work
for the *Tribune,* and I do sort of and sometimes, but she must
have thought I was on assignment. I decided to play along.

"Well, let's begin with your dinner dance," I said.

"Of course, it's just one of our three big annual fund-
raisers." She told me about the other two in considerable detail, and then about the dinner dance itself, the silent auction,
the raffles, how the theme is chosen, the committee, how
much money was raised for the hospital. I took notes and
was happy that I'd thought to bring a notebook and pen.

"Well," I said finally, "you've given me a lot to work with."

"I hope so. You can never get too much publicity. Any
idea when your article might run?"

"I'm sorry. I just write them. The editors fit them in. Since
this is about your whole program, not just the one event, I
suppose they might even hold it until . . . what's coming up?
Your fall outing?"

"That might be nice. That wouldn't be bad at all," she said.

"May I ask you a question?" I unfolded the photograph
of Lisa Kim's parents taken at the last dinner dance which I'd
torn from the newspaper, and smoothed it out in front of her.
"I picked this out of the files, and I just wondered . . ."

"Oh, that's Dr. Kim and Dr. Kim, our Korean couple. We're so pleased with them. He's a radiologist and she's a pediatrician. Very, very competent."

"And this gentleman?" I asked. "He looks so familiar to me."

"Let's see. Oh, that's Dr. Decarre. Albert Decarre."

"And is he a radiologist or . . . ?"

"No, no. He's a psychiatrist," she said.

That morning I sat on Carolyn's deck a long time looking at his phone number in the phone book. Up until now, everything could be rewound and erased. After this I wasn't quite so sure. I took the dogs down to the dog beach at Belmont Harbor and threw sticks for them; I went through the dialogue—especially my half—in my mind. I went home and wrote it down. In the afternoon I bought a prepaid cell phone with cash; I filled out the forms using a fictitious name and address. I bought some Diet Dr Pepper and put three cans on ice. Just before I called, I opened one.

"Dr. Decarre?" I asked.

"Speaking."

"My name is David Lester. I'm a freelance writer and I'm working on an article for the *Chicago Tribune* about the death of the actress Lisa Kim. Our article is going to state that an eyewitness saw you with Ms. Kim a few minutes before the accident occurred. Do you have any reaction to that claim?"

"What? No. No, no."

"We are also going to print that you had a personal relationship with Ms. Kim. Can you confirm or deny this?"

"Lisa Kim was a family friend. I've been friends of her parents for many years. I'd known Lisa since she was a child. That's all."

"Paul? What is it, dear?" a voice asked in the background.

"Nothing. Just the hospital." I jerked my head up. He had just lied. Why had he just lied?

"We're ready to serve," the voice said.

"I'll be right there," Decarre said.

"Dr. Decarre, how long was Lisa Kim a patient of yours?" I asked.

"I can neither confirm nor deny that anyone is or was a patient of mine. It is a violation of the Illinois Mental Health and Developmental Disabilities Confidentiality Code to do so."

"Would you like at this time to make any statement, clarify or add information to the article?" I asked. "We would be happy to represent your point of view."

There was a long pause. "No."

"Thank you for your time," I said and hung up. The son of a bitch had lied, and he hadn't denied that Lisa had been his patient. And if he was a longtime family friend, why didn't Tanya Kim recognize him in the photograph? That didn't make sense.

My phone rang, and it was Lydia. Charlie Duke had called her out of the blue. "He's in Kansas seeing his family. He wants to visit us."

"What? Didn't you tell him?"

"Of course I told him. I said, 'Charlie, you need to know that Pete and I aren't living together right now.'" I don't think either of us had really said it before. I wondered if it had been hard, and if she had rehearsed saying the words, as I probably would have.

"Do you know what he said?" she asked.

"What?"

"He said, 'Oh you poor kids. That seals it. I'll be right there.'" I laughed. I heard her laugh.

"So when's he coming?" I asked.

"Tomorrow."

"Tomorrow? Oh Jesus, Lydia, I'm not sure I can do this."

"Well, he's coming. I'll handle this if you can't." Lydia's answers sometimes reminded me of wines. They had tiny hints of martyrdom with the suggestion of moral superiority and guilt infliction.

I went to see Rosalie Belcher Svigos again on my way to pick Charlie up at the bus station. First I called her cell phone, gambling that she wouldn't pick up, and she didn't. I left a cryptic little message. Would be in the hospital at 10:00 tomorrow morning. Know the name of the guy in Lisa's car. Rosalie called me three times and I didn't pick up. The third time she left a message to meet her at a certain nurses' station on the eleventh floor. Good. I wanted to see her face when I said his name.

I was on time and so was she. "Who is he?" she said immediately.

"Albert Decarre. I think he was Lisa's psychiatrist and her lover."

"Fuck!" she said. "Son of a bitch. I was afraid something like this was going on." She took me into a family-counseling room and sat down hard in a chair. She wanted to know my evidence, and I laid it out for her. I told her about the photograph and phone call. I told her about his lie and his nondenial. I did not tell her about the hypnosis. She shook her head. "What makes you think they were lovers?" she asked.

"Lisa wrote—but for some reason didn't send—a letter addressed to P, 'P' period." I took the letter from my hip pocket and gave it to her. She slowly and carefully read it twice.

"Wow," she said. "How'd you get this."

"Maud gave it to me thinking I was P. I gave it to an old boyfriend of Lisa's named Peter Carey, thinking he was P; he said it wasn't for him. Then who was it meant for? When I was talking to Decarre on the phone, his wife came in and called him 'Paul'; he goes by 'Paul.' Maybe it's far-fetched, but I started playing around with it, and it's not too hard to get from 'Paul Decarre' to 'P. Decarre' to 'de Carre' if you frenchify it to 'Peter Carey'?"

"Not so far-fetched," said Rosalie. Apparently Lisa gave everyone she knew a nickname or called them by their initials. Rosalie said I would have been "P" or "Mr. P" or "PF Flyer" or "Old Shoe" or who knows. She also said that she had always felt something wasn't right about Lisa's death, had always known it, but couldn't find even a shred of evidence, so when I called, she'd agreed to see me out of desperation; I was the first person to share her suspicion. It was the timing of the whole thing that bothered her. Lisa had called her a few weeks earlier to say that she was very, very in love, but she wouldn't say with whom. Both those things were unlike her; she usually let other people fall in love with her, and she always told Rosalie everything. And there was the movie she'd been cast in. She was very excited about it. She was working hard on the role and making plans to go to New York. She was running every day and taking megavitamin shots. She'd never felt happier or better. It was, said Rosalie, an anti-coincidence, and she didn't believe in coincidences of any kind. Then there was the whole heroin thing. "It just didn't fit," Rosalie said. "It wasn't Lisa. It wasn't right. Let's look this guy up." She went out into the hall and came back pulling a computer on a cart. I looked over her shoulder. He'd gone to a good med school, been in a top-notch residency program. His clinical interests were depression, drug abuse, eating disorders, marital problems, phobias, sexual dysfunctions, sex therapy.

"Maybe they all say that," I said.

We looked at two other psychiatrists on the staff. They had entirely different areas of specialization. "Let me look at something else," said Rosalie. "Listen to this. Accordng to the Illinois Department of Professional Regulation, Dr. Albert Decarre has been reprimanded for professional misconduct."

"What does that mean?" I asked.

"Don't know," Rosalie said, "but it could include having a relationship with a patient."

"So he may have done this before?"

"Possibly. He's done something. What you really need to know is whether Lisa was his patient." She said that she couldn't help me with that because that information would be in the doctor's records, not the hospital's. When I told her Decarre had a stiff back and asked if she could find out about it, she said only if he'd had surgery, and then depending on where the surgery had been performed. She said she'd try.

Her eyes swept by me like spotlights at a grand opening. "If this guy," she said, "if this guy. . . ." Then she focused on me. "What else are you trying to find out?"

I told her I needed to know Lisa's mother's maiden name and Lisa's Social Security number.

"Dr. Kim's maiden name is Sam. The Social Security number I don't know, but I might be able to find out. Lisa stayed with us for two weeks when she was between apartments and left a lot of stuff. Let me look at it; I might find a check stub or something."

I told her I didn't understand the line, "You can say that our little friend helped . . ." I was afraid it might be a reference to drugs. "What else could it be?"

"Maybe the megavitamins, and those are prescription. I bet you this guy was writing scripts for her."

There was a time when Charlie Duke could have stepped off that bus as if it were a Learjet, but this day he looked about like everyone else who had come from Topeka by Greyhound, and that wasn't very good. His linen slacks were badly wrinkled, his guayabera shirt could not hide that he'd grown thicker and softer in the middle, his gray hair had a yellowish cast to it, and there was a road map of fine red capillaries on his nose. Then, when he smiled, I saw that the long white roots of his teeth were exposed. "Periodontal disease," he would say. "Awful stuff. Going to lose them all. Oh well." But that was later.

Charlie tossed one long arm around my shoulders and kissed me on the forehead; there was a time when he could have pulled that off, too. "You poor kids," he said. "I just can't imagine. You'll have to tell me all about it." I never did, and he never brought it up again.

I gave him the Cook's tour of the city: Printer's Row, University of Chicago, the Adler Planetarium with skyline view (Charlie took several pictures with an ancient-but-immaculate Instamatic camera), the Loop, the lakefront, and Millennium Park. Charlie made a big deal about having to visit "the legendary Billy Goat Tavern," and I knew what that was about. He needed a drink. He'd been drinking when I picked him up although it was barely noon, and I grimaced at the thought of Charlie on a bus with a pint in a brown bag.

The Billy Goat is underneath Michigan Avenue and the Tribune Tower surrounded by loading docks. It claims to have once been the hangout of writers and reporters from the city's newspapers, and their autographed photos are all over the walls, but these are old and faded now, and its customers are mostly tourists who know the place from John Belushi's "cheeseborger, cheeseborger" skit. Charlie had a shot and a beer; I was able to negotiate my way down to a beer alone. When I kidded him about "riding the dog," he said it was better than Flecha Roja.

"Flecha Roja?" I said. "Don't tell me you took buses all the way from Mexico City."

"From Cuernavaca. Actually from Tepoztlán. Father Dick was at a retreat, and Mr. John Handy (Charlie's name for his twenty-year-old Ford) needs a new clutch at the moment, so I even rode the local into town." Twice during his years in Mexico, Charlie had used hard work and good investment to accumulate some modest wealth, but each time he had awakened one morning to discover that the peso had been devalued while he slept, and his money was worth a fraction of what it had been worth the day before. It is the plight of the Mexican middle class which always seems to pay the price for the greed, corruption, and mismanagement of those in power. The very wealthy aren't much bothered, and the very poor haven't much to lose (staples such as beans, rice, corn, and the diesel fuel that powers the old school buses poor people ride everywhere have traditionally been subsidized), but the always-fledgling middle class takes it on the chin every time.

Charlie and I met Lydia at our old place. He put his arms around her and held her to him for several moments; she smiled at me beneath his arm. The apartment seemed bare to me, although I couldn't identify a single thing that was missing or changed. It smelled a little different. We had a drink, and Lydia and Charlie talked. I watched Lydia. She had a new haircut that was stylish and looked expensive. She was tan. Odd. I had always owned the sun and Lydia the shade. She had lost a little weight.

Charlie insisted on treating us to dinner, so we went to La Choza because it was nearby, inexpensive, Mexican, BYO, and the BYO was just beer and wine. By dinnertime Charlie was half in the bag, and I was confused about how that was happening in front of me; he must have been sneaking drinks when he went to the bathroom. We sat in the garden of the restaurant beneath the El tracks and the twinkling, year-round Christmas lights, drank cold Tecates against the heat, and ate enchiladas and arroz con pollo. Charlie told funny stories about the local men he had hired to dig a small swimming pool in his garden. After three years of frustration, he gave up and converted it into a septic tank. He told a troubling story about how he had discovered a method for converting grain alcohol into vodka, and another about two village boys named Pedro and Pablito who had taken to hanging out at the ranch, doing Charlie's chores and running his errands. He spoke of them several times and quite fondly, so that a suspicion hatched in my mind that they might be doing other things for him, or at least stealing from him. And, of course, he told his usual quotient of improbable tales about unlikely characters doing barely believable things. In one of these an over-the-hill Mexican soap-opera star had lost her luxury villa in a backgammon game but not its detached garage, which had a separate deed. All she had left was her '68 Mercedes convertible, so she married her chauffeur and they were living in the car in the garage. To the chagrin of the municipal government, no one could find anything illegal with the arrangement.

Then there was "Arturo, the lout, a BMW Bolshevik if there ever was one. Everyone knew his father bought him the position at UNAM to begin with, and of course Sylvia left him years ago, sick to death of his philandering. So, after all those years of ranting and raving about the revolution ad nauseam, guess what? They threw him out of the university, and guess why? Not lefty enough. Now, isn't that just a hoot?"

"Charlie," I said, "I don't have any idea who you are talking about and never have. I just don't know any of these people."

"I don't know half of them myself," he said. "It doesn't

really matter. It's just talk." If you sifted through Charlie's pa-
laver and listened carefully enough, you could almost always
find some small truth, and this was one of them: "It's just
talk." I laughed aloud.

We had emptied our cooler of beer, and I asked for the
check and went to the bathroom, but when I got back, Charlie had somehow produced a bottle of red wine and was in the
process of opening it. It occurred to me as he madly popped
the cork that he had built the evening to this pinnacle of artificial gaiety primarily so he could drink some more. Walking
back to Lydia's car a bit later, Charlie was unsteady on his
legs and went on and on about "what a marvelous evening"
it had been.

As soon as we stumbled into the apartment, Charlie put
on blue cotton pajamas with navy piping and went to sleep
on the couch. Lydia and I had a discussion about whether
or not I should drive, although we both knew we were really
talking about something else. I think we were feeling the
closeness that divorced parents feel when they have to deal
with a wayward or ill child, and we were hoping that it was
something a little more.

"Stay," she said. "Don't take the chance."

"I would, but for the dogs."

"When did you walk them?"

"Just before we came over."

"They should be fine until morning. And if they aren't,
so what?" We went to bed, but it didn't work. Lydia did all the
things I had always wanted her to do, but it still didn't work.
It was too hot, we were too sticky, and Charlie began to snore.
I said I was self-conscious. Lydia said she was, too. I made

the *Macbeth* joke about drink: "It provokes the desire, but it takes away the performance." Lydia was defiantly cheerful. We tried to just hold each other. We were all wrong-handed.

Finally I said, "Listen, I'm feeling guilty about those dogs. I don't think I can sleep. I think I'd better go."

"Well, sure, I mean, if you can't sleep." I went down the stairs as fast as I could. I was still a little drunk and already a little hung over. I sat in the car trying to think of a moment in my life when I had felt worse. I wondered if Lydia was feeling this awful. God, I'd never wanted to want someone so much in my life. "Christ," I said out loud, "Jesus Christ. What have I done? Can this possibly be about Lisa Kim?" I had stepped outside for just a moment just to look around, and it seemed that the door had closed and locked behind me. I had an uneasy feeling, which I wanted very much to deny, that I had entered a new part of life, one in which everything was not a beginning; there were now some endings. Everything was not falling in love, there was now falling *out* of love. I had never really known that was possible.

When I picked Charlie up the next day to take him back to the bus station, he was rooting around in the kitchen cabinets. "Any idea where Lydia keeps the hooch?" he asked. "I need a tiny bracer, hair of the dog."

I showed him the hutch in the living room where the liquor was, and he had a large, quick drink.

"There. Much better."

At the bus he held me as long and as hard as he had held Lydia the night before. I could feel his heart beating, or mine; I knew that I'd probably never see him again. It wasn't a premonition or anything like that; it was just a bit of knowledge:

Our time had passed. Our stars had crossed—his and Lydia's and mine—and I was very happy that they had, but that was all over. Our vectors were speeding away from each other. As had happened so often lately, I had a sense of transition and inevitability. There is so much that is beyond our control, all you can really do is deal with that which isn't. That which wasn't seemed to be Lisa Kim.

"Were you in love with her?" asks the girl, whose hair is now pink. "That is, if she ever really existed which, of course, she didn't, blah blah blah."

"I guess I was, in some way," I answer.

"That's pretty weird," she says.

"Why?"

"She doesn't exist, and then she died, so she doesn't exist squared."

"But she *did* exist," I say.

"Not for you. Might as well be fiction," says Nick.

"People fall in love with fictional characters all the time."

"Fourteen-year-old girls with rock singers," says Nick.

"No, everyone. All of us. I'll give you an example. When I was your age, a little older, I was in college, I fell in love with a beautiful tomboy named Elena, and she fell in love with me, or so I thought, and it all happened one spring day in the backyard of one of my professor's houses on a hilltop over-looking the university. White clouds were moving fast across a blue sky, our bare feet touched in the new grass, and it was thrilling, truly thrilling."

"Oh boy, Mr. Ferry got lucky."

"Spare us the details, please," said the girl with pink hair.

"No," I go on, "this wasn't about sex. This was about love. I told her everything that was in my heart, and she listened to me intently; I knew she did, and I fell in love. A year later, I bought a ring, and the night I was going to give it to her and ask her to marry me and spend the rest of her life with me, I evoked the memory of that spring afternoon that for me was the very foundation stone of our relationship. And you know what she remembered of it?"

"What?"

"She remembered being chilly. She remembered that the grass was damp and she got cold. That was it. I probed and probed, but that was it. I never gave her the ring. I kept it in my pocket."

"What's your point?" asks the dog-faced boy.

"My point is that I'd fallen in love with a fictional character. I'd made her up."

"I think that your love was fictional," says the pink-haired girl. "I think that had you really loved her, you would have forgiven her. I think that what you felt was infatuation, rather than love."

"Maybe. Probably," I say, "but didn't someone in here once say that infatuation is a form of love?"

"I think it's a stage of love," says the pink-haired girl. "An early stage."

"My point is that love is like sex; some big part of it is in your mind."

"I refuse to believe that," says someone.

"He might be right," says the dog-faced boy. "I read an article on a survey someone did that said for some high percentage of people—most of us, if I recall correctly—no actual sexual experience has ever lived up to what you thought it would be before you ever had sex at all."

"That's pretty scary," says the pink-haired girl.

"But isn't that true of anything?" says Nick. "Wouldn't it be true of anything, I mean, like cheeseburgers or whatever? You never think of a cheeseburger that's dry and cold, do you? Just hot and juicy. I think you're really talking about the real versus the ideal."

"How do you mean?"

"Well, love or sex or whatever, if you imagine it, you're going to imagine it in its most perfect form. I mean, if I say 'summer day,' you think of the perfect summer day, not a chilly, rainy one."

"Okay. What is ideal love, then?" I ask.

"The love of a dog," says the pink-haired girl without hesitation.

"Oh Christ," says someone.

"No, I'm serious. You can laugh at old ladies with cats, but think about it."

"Think about what?"

"Think about the love a pet gives you," says the pink-haired girl.

"Okay, I'll think about it. It's submissive and extremely limited," says Nick.

"Of course it's limited. I'm not being sappy here—"

"Okay, it's unconditional—"

"It's unconditional, and it doesn't change," says the pink-haired girl. "It's static. It doesn't evolve. A pet and its master don't grow apart and don't go their separate ways. A pet doesn't have a friggin' midlife crisis and run off with his friggin' sales assistant . . ."

"Oh Christ," says someone. "I *thought* this is where we were headed."

"Well, I can't help it. The only time a pet hurts you is when it dies."

"Which it will do about seven times in your lifetime," says the dog-faced boy.

"Also, a pet doesn't grow up and need to reject you like a kid," says the pink-haired girl.

"You're going to be one of those people with a home full of dogs they call the health department on," says Nick.

"I know I am."

"But what about real love?" asks someone.

"What's that?" asks the pink-haired girl.

"Romantic love. Love between a man and a woman."

"Or a man and a man or a woman and a woman," says someone.

"Case in point," I say. "Now we make sure to include and honor homosexuals. A hundred years ago we chased them out of town or killed them. Fifty years ago we put them in hospitals, and sometimes they killed themselves. Now we have parades for them. What's changed besides perception?"

"Yeah," says Nick cautiously, "but there's a difference between perception and fantasy. I mean, this Lisa Kim is pure fantasy."

"I put it to you that many of the most celebrated loves in literature were at least partly fantasy. Romeo and Juliet. How many days did they know each other? How many total minutes were they together? 'I was a child and she was a child,/In this kingdom by the sea,/But we loved with a love that was more than love—I and my Annabel Lee.'"

"Who's that?" asks Nick.

"Poe. Take Lenore, for that matter," I say.

"But those are lost loves," says Nick. "They at least existed. There's a difference between the remembered and the imaginary."

"How about 'The Lady of Shalott?'" I ask. "Do you guys know 'The Lady of Shalott'? Nick, grab *Sound and Sense* behind you. Is it in there?"

"No."

"Grab the *Norton*. I know it's in there."

"Here it is."

"Run across the hall and make some copies, would you?"

"How about Odysseus?" says someone. "He's gone for twenty years, during which time he says no to immortality, says no to living with a beautiful, sexy goddess on a desert island because he's so in love with his wife, and when he finally gets home she doesn't even recognize him."

"But who does?" asks the girl with pink hair. "Do you remember who does? His old dog does. I rest my case."

"Yeah, but then the old dog dies on a pile of shit," says the dog-faced boy.

"So he's gone twenty years," says someone. "He's home one night, and then he says he has to go see his father and then he has to take another journey, for God's sake. What about Penelope is Odysseus in love with? And what is she in love with?"

"Nick, pass those out. Everyone read 'The Lady of Shalott' for tomorrow. Here's the question: What's she in love with?"

I stopped to get a big tablet of newsprint and then went back to Carolyn's place to get to work. I put both extra leaves in her big Mission-style dining-room table and pulled it into the middle of the living room beneath a skylight and facing the longest interior wall, from which I removed Carolyn's artwork. I put the dining chairs in the spare bedroom and brought in Carolyn's office chair. I set up my laptop and stacked my notebooks and files. Then I started making lists in Magic Marker on the newsprint and taping these to the long wall. I made a list of everything that I knew. I made a list of everything I suspected and a list of everything that I did not know in the form of questions. The first and foremost of these was, "Was Lisa Decarre's patient?" I made three time-lines; one for the day of Lisa's death, one for the preceding thirty days, and one for the preceding one hundred eighty days. I made a sheet for each of the major players and on it I listed everything I knew about that person. I made a list of all the people I'd encountered with phone numbers, addresses, and e-mail info. When Rosalie called with Lisa's Social Security number, I wrote that large on its own sheet. I wrote some scripts of imagined conversations—at least, my half of them. Finally, I wrote down a list of things to do and, in the days ahead, I did them.

I rented a post-office box. I took out ads in the little weekly newspapers up and down the North Shore in an effort to locate other patients of Dr. Decarre's. I called the Psychology Department at Northwestern University and had a nice chat with the secretary there. I gave her a cock-and-bull story about representing a company that had developed a series of new personality-assessment tools and was looking for grad students to test them "for $35 an hour. Do you think anyone in your program might be interested?"

"Oh, I think so." I found out that I could send or bring materials to the office to distribute in student mailboxes, and I found out the names of the two students in the pro-gram who had off-campus mailboxes. One of these was all I needed: Geoffrey Hand.

I called Mike Peoples. He and I had been in the English Ph.D. program at Northwestern, and at one time we had been interested in the same minor Lake District poet; he decided to study the guy, and I decided not to. He became a scholar, and I became a teacher. The absurdities of academic eco-nomics being what they are, that allowed me to bow out with a Masters degree so that I could start competing for fairly-high-paying high school teaching jobs, and it allowed him to pay two more years of upper-end tuition and write a dis-sertation before he could start competing for fairly-low-pay-ing college-teaching jobs. He did have an office in University Library, however, and that was another thing I needed.

Although some years had passed since we'd been in school together, we seemed always to revert to that particular brand of grad-student repartee that is a lot like shower-room towel snapping. He liked to call me "the common man" and "an unsung hero in the trenches of the war on ignorance and ignominy," and I liked to ask if he was still masturbating in the stacks. This time I also said, "How's the book going?"

"Pretty damn good. I'm almost finished. I read a chapter

at St. Andrews last spring, and I'm reading the last chapter at the MLA in December."

I asked Mike if I could use his carrel once or twice for private meetings.

"Of course. No problem. Just call me the day before and buy me a pint of Guinness at your convenience."

"It's a deal."

"Anything I can do to help the common man."

When Carolyn called, I couldn't find my calendar in the swirl of papers on my desktop; I was sure I'd lost track of time and she was due home the next day, or she'd aborted the trip for one reason or another. "No, we just got these cheap phone cards, so we've been calling everyone, and we thought we'd call you and see how Cooper is. Actually, we're still in Italy."

It was a good thing. Her living space had taken on the appearance of a command post, with furniture pushed to the side and her paintings and prints stacked against the wall. There were piles everywhere—clothing, newspapers, telephone books, some dishes. Now all the walls were covered with taped lists on newsprint, and two big window fans, one drawing air in the front, one pushing it out the back, caused these to ripple and billow like so many sails in my secret little regatta.

"Everything okay?" she asked.

"Absolutely!" I told her about the dogs, about our morning walks to the dog beach and evenings on the deck. I told her about Lydia and Charlie. Finally I told her about Lisa Kim and Decarre, that he was a psychiatrist and that he'd been disciplined once before. Then I said, "Now listen to this:

He was with her in her car minutes before the crash. Also, the autopsy report shows that she had opiates in her system, and her best friend says no way would she ever use heroin."

"Which means what?" Carolyn asked.

"Codeine or morphine, maybe."

"I see. And who has access to morphine?"

"Right." Neither of us spoke for a long moment.

"There's something that isn't right here, isn't there?" she said.

"I think so," I said.

"I'm going to assume that everything you've told me here is true and verifiable."

"Everything I've told you is true. Not quite everything is verifiable, at least not yet."

"I'm thinking maybe you should go to the police," she said.

"Do you think I have enough?" I asked.

"I'm not sure. You have something, but I don't know anything about criminal law. Just go ask the cops. Or go see Officer Lotts."

I had finally found my calendar. "Hey, what are you doing in Italy? I thought you were supposed to be in Greece by now."

"Well, we met a couple of Italian guys," she said. "Aldo and Luca."

Wendy was in love with Aldo, and Luca was in love with Carolyn. "Zee Irish woman," he would say, "is zee better woman of zee world." She told me about bobbing through Siena traffic on the back of a Vespa, about a weekend at Aldo's family farm in the Tuscan countryside, about visiting some

Etruscan ruins so far off the path that they were the only people there, about evenings of candlelight, pasta, and wine.

"This sounds serious," I said.

"Not really. A few weeks and it will all be over."

"Are you sad?"

"No," she said, "he's not the guy." Besides, she was finally tired of traveling, had been away long enough, was anxious to start her new job. "That's another reason for my call. I think I'll be home on September 15," she said.

We talked some logistics. We didn't talk about where I would go on September 15.

Dorothy Murrell's voice was as plaintive and precise as a stringed instrument, and she spoke with the caution of someone walking on new ice. I told her my name was Geoffrey Hand. "You responded to my newspaper advertisement . . ."

"Oh, yes. I see. Okay . . ."

I said that I had a few more questions, and I wondered if I might be able to meet her. She thought not. She thought that she'd said all she wanted to say in her letter. I suggested a public place. "University Library, for instance. I have access to a carrel there."

"Are you a student at the university?" she asked.

"I am a graduate student in psychology," I lied. I told her I was gathering information for my dissertation, and that her letter was exactly what I was looking for.

She interrupted. "I won't identify him. I will not identify him."

I explained that unless she did, nothing could really be done.

"I don't care," she said. "I will not do that to him. It would crush him. I cannot hurt him like that."

When I finally accepted her terms, she agreed, albeit a bit reluctantly, to meet me in the reference room of the library at 10:00 A.M. on Saturday.

"I'll wear a yellow baseball cap," I said.

I was sitting at the table staring at my lists on the wall when Lydia called. Her car had broken down halfway between Chicago and Milwaukee. "Is there any possible way—"

" 'Course. I'll come get you. I'll be glad to."

She was sitting on her briefcase working on her laptop in front of the gas station when I pulled up. She was thinner and tanner, and now she had some highlights in her hair. She was wearing a suit and high heels. "My goodness," I said, "if I didn't know better, I'd think you were someone important." It was a joke, but it was a bad one, and I knew it as soon as I'd said it; she treated it as a joke.

"Shut up," she said. "My God, what a day!" Her battery light had come on on the highway, and then all the dash lights, and then the car had died going full speed. She had gotten it onto the shoulder, and a nice guy had stopped and tried to give her a jump, but it had not taken, so she had had the car towed and it's the alternator, but the guy can't get to it until tomorrow morning. She told it all like that, a bit breathlessly.

I said that I'd bring her back the next day to pick it up if she wanted me to.

"Oh God, that would be wonderful," she said. "I don't know how else I'll get out here."

I liked that she was nervous; I found it a little titillating. It was as if we were on a little date. I had even showered quickly and put on a clean shirt, one that she had given me.

Suddenly I realized what I had been doing; I'd been waiting. I'd been waiting for a feeling that I had once had and somehow lost. This made me feel better because it meant that I wasn't just stringing her along, and I wasn't just afraid to leave her or hurt her. And if that morning didn't exactly give me the feeling, it at least gave me hope that it was still within me or within us. I told a dumb joke and she laughed. I told another.

She told me that she had gotten a nice letter from Charlie that was addressed to both of us. I was a little bothered that it had come to her; I was sure I'd given him my address at Carolyn's place. "So, what did it say?" I asked.

"I'll give it to you when we get home."

"Can't you just tell me?"

"Not really. You can read it yourself." She started to laugh.

"What?" I asked.

"There's something in there about a one-legged flamenco dancer named Paco Paco," she said. She was laughing harder.

"What?" I was laughing now, too.

"I loved it when you said, 'Charlie I've never known any of these people . . .'" She was laughing too hard to finish. I was, too. We couldn't stop for a couple of minutes. When we finally did, she said, "And when he said he didn't know most of them either . . ." That started us again. We were on the highway doing seventy-five and laughing so hard, I was afraid we'd crash into someone or something. There was a car running parallel to us and a woman in the passenger seat watching us with a look of horror on her face.

I touched Lydia's arm. "Look," I said to her. That started us a third time. When we finally settled down and wiped our eyes, the woman was gone and we were approaching the toll plaza. "She probably thought we were crying," I said.

"Oh Lord." She stopped her laughter this time. "My God."

"Hey," I said. "Have you eaten? I'm starving."

"I could eat something," she said.

"Burger King okay?"

"Sure." For a long time, we'd ordered the same thing: two chicken whoppers, no mayo, one order of onion rings, and a vanilla shake. We'd split the rings, put them on our sandwiches, and share the milkshake. That's what we did that day. Afterward she was quiet.

"You okay?" I asked.

"Yes."

"Aren't you going to finish that?" I asked. Her sandwich was half eaten.

"No. You want it?"

"Well . . ."

When I dropped her off, I said, "What's wrong?"

"Nothing," she said. We both forgot about Charlie's letter.

"About the third time I saw him, he said 'Call me Paul,'" said Jeanette Landrow. "Very California, I thought. What a red flag!" She laughed. "Oh God, I should have seen it coming, but . . ." She laughed again. "Anyway!"

She was a pretty, dark-haired woman with a straight, thin nose, a wide mouth, and very large black eyes who had sent me a timid, tentative letter. We were sitting on either side of and at either end of a picnic table in a park by Lake Michigan. We could see joggers and bikers on the path across the way, but we were alone. There was a breeze off the water, and Jeanette was looking at the big paper cup of coffee I had brought her.

"So, it was probably in the next session that he told me that the reason I was having problems sustaining relationships was because I had unresolved issues with my father, who had left when I was six and when he was the only man I knew, and it was some form of arrested development. Well, it all made perfect sense to me, and he said he could help me. For a while we had very productive sessions and I was very excited. I was really getting somewhere.

"Then, about the tenth time I saw him, he said kind of out of the blue not to be alarmed if I started to feel attracted to him, that this is a common phenomenon that happens as trust develops between a patient and a therapist; and that if it were to happen to me, he wanted me to know that it was normal and just not to worry about it. In fact he said it could even be a good thing, that sometimes patients are able to explore their phobias and desires—I remember thinking it was odd that he used the word 'desires'—in the safety of the therapeutic relationship, that using the therapist as both a guide and guinea pig, they can learn to trust, they can learn healthy ways of sharing and giving and so on, and then the therapist can help them bring the treatment to a conclusion and move beyond it, apply all this stuff in their lives, and so on. The hard part about all of this is that he's very good at his job. Very, very good. He really helped me—for a while, at least. Helped me to learn how to compromise without setting up resentment. Taught me where the line is between myself and the other person, something I'd always had trouble with. Taught me how to recognize and state my needs. Taught me how to say no in a reasonable, healthy way; all of this seems so ironic now. Taught me how to negotiate. Then," she took a deep breath and laughed again. "Oh God, this is so hard."

"Would you like to stop?" I asked.

"No, no. I need to tell someone. It might as well be you. By that I mean a stranger. Someone who's objective. Just do me one favor. Just look that way. Just don't look at me, okay?"

"Sure." For thirty or forty minutes, as she talked, I wrote. I didn't look up, but later in the parking lot, I did look at her and smile and thank her and say, "May I ask you one question?"

"Yes."

"Have you ever thought about reporting this?"

"Yes. I know I should. I really know that I should."

When I got home, there was a message from Rosalie on the answering machine: "Six years ago Decarre had a lumbar fusion at L4 and L5, which would greatly limit the flexibility of his lower back."

I had found two more pieces of the puzzle, but I was still missing the one right in the middle that interlocked with half a dozen others: Was Lisa Decarre's patient? I had a plan for finding out, but it was tricky and iffy, and I'd get only one shot at it. If it didn't work, I might never find out, and if I never found out, none of this was going anywhere. Again I got up early and took the dogs to the beach. Again I wrote the script in my head and then on paper. Again I opened a Diet Dr Pepper and used the prepaid cell phone.

"Customer service."

"I'm wondering if you can help me with a discrepancy between our records and a doctor's records," I said.

"I'll do my best. Can you give me an account number?"

"Will a Social Security number do?" I gave her Lisa's and identified myself as Lisa's father.

"I'm sorry, but all account information and medical records are confidential. Now if you have Lisa Kim call us, we'll be happy to help her."

"I know this is going to make you feel terrible, but Lisa is deceased. She was killed in a car accident."

"Oh gosh, I see it now. I'm so sorry . . ."

We each apologized a couple of times. I talked about tying up loose ends. I said Lisa had been billed for a doctor's appointment we were certain she hadn't kept, and we wanted to know if the insurance company had been billed, too, and paid its portion.

The woman on the phone said that she would help me, but it was a violation of law and policy; she could lose her job. "All I am allowed to say to any unauthorized inquiry is, 'I have no information on that individual.' That's all I can say."

"Are you allowed to *not* say, 'I have no information on that individual'?"

"What do you mean?" she asked.

"Can you just say nothing?" I asked.

"Well . . ."

"I mean, suppose I ask the question, and suppose you *do* have information on the patient; can you remain silent?"

"Well, I don't know. I suppose . . ."

"If I give you a date of an office visit, and you don't have any information, then you answer that you have no information, right?"

"Right."

"What if I give you a date, and you *do* have information; can you say nothing?"

She was confused. She stalled. She asked if I could verify that I was Lisa's father, and asked me Lisa's street address, phone number, and mother's maiden name. I dutifully read these from the sheet of newsprint labeled "Lisa's Vital Statistics."

She paused. "Okay, I'll try it."

"Thank you very much. I really appreciate this. Can you tell me if Lisa saw Dr. Albert Decarre on Tuesday, December 4?" I asked.

"I have no information on that individual," she said.

"How about on November 27?"

"I have no information . . . listen, this sounds like you're fishing. I can't—"

"I know, I know. Just one more, I promise. Just one more. How about on Tuesday, November 20?"

I did not hear an answer. "Are you still there?"

"Still here," she said.

"Okay, then. Thank you very much," I said.

"You're welcome."

I hung up the phone and whooped. I drained the Dr Pepper. The son of a bitch had been treating her. He had seen her on November 24, just before Thanksgiving and just about when she'd written the letter. What had happened to prevent her from sending it may have happened in that session.

I looked at the clock. An hour until I was to pick up Lydia. I went into the bathroom and ran the shower. The phone rang and it was Lydia. She said she had another ride.

"But you said you had no way—"

"Pete."

"Yes."

There was a pause. Then she said carefully, "That was too hard for me yesterday. I can't do that anymore. It was that dumb sandwich. I gotta go."

"Wait, Lydia, wait a minute."

"Can't. They're here for me."

"What about Charlie's letter?" But the phone was dead. I went back to the bathroom and turned off the shower. I sat on the deck. I could remember living with Lydia, but I could not imagine doing it again. It all seemed past tense. I had a strange sense of something like emotional gravity weighing at me, pulling me down. I went back in the living room to the "things to do" list. I added this: Look for an apartment.

Then I lay down on the floor.

11

. . .

BACK TO SCHOOL

THE LAST TIME I'd seen Steve Lotts had been at Wendy and Carolyn's good-bye party, and he'd walked away in what looked a lot like disgust. Despite Carolyn's suggestion, I had no intention of calling him. Strangely, he called me instead. Of course, it wasn't strange at all. I found out later that Carolyn had talked to him right after she had talked to me and told him that I might be on to something after all, and that I needed some advice.

Steve suggested we eat lunch at his favorite place, the North Pond Café in Lincoln Park. He was waiting for me over a glass of pinot grigio since it was his first day off in a while. I had one, too, since it was nearly my last day off. A front had come down the lake and cleaned the city out; it was clear and almost cool for the first time in weeks, cool enough that you knew for the first time that summer would not last forever.

As always, Steve had chosen the perfect table. We were look-ing out across the pond and the trees to the skyline.

"You gotta try this thing, this asparagus-mushroom-cream tart. Unbelievable," he said. He didn't mention the words we had exchanged at the ball game or at the dinner, and he didn't mention Lydia. I filled him in on Albert Decarre.

"He lied to her. He lied to his own wife," I said.

"Oh, like what else is new. I mean, how many guys *don't* lie to their wives? Exactly why I'm not married."

"Why would he tell her it was the hospital calling?"

"So he wouldn't have to say he was being exposed or threatened or blackmailed or slandered," he said. "So he wouldn't ruin her dinner party? I don't know, or maybe he was boinking this Korean chick, and he had something to hide. Doesn't mean he killed her, Pete."

"There's an eyewitness. I'm an eyewitness. I saw him get out of the goddamn car with my own two eyes."

Steve said a bad drunken lawyer would take me apart on the stand over that.

"You don't think I'd make a credible witness?" I asked.

"It's not that. It's all the other stuff. It's dark. It's raining. You don't remember this guy for seven months, and then only under hypnosis. Yikes. Hypnosis makes juries nervous. Hocus-pocus. Besides, there's your personal stake in all of this. I'm sorry, Pete, but—"

"I mean it almost sounds as if you think I'm making all of this up," I said.

"Of course not. I believe the guy was there. I believe he was involved in the girl's death. He could have at least prevented it, and it's possible he caused it. He's mixed up in it some-how, but that's just my belief. Believing and proving are two different things, and frankly you just don't have any evidence at all."

"So how do I get evidence?"

"I'm not sure you do." He shrugged. "It's an imperfect sci-ence. Fifty percent of major crimes are never solved. Fifty percent of criminals get away with it, and believe me a lot of criminals are really dumb. God knows what percent of the smart ones get away with it, and this doctor of yours is smart."

"But he's guilty."

"So's O. J. You know it, and I know it, but . . ." He shrugged his shoulders. "Like I said, its an imperfect science."

"So that's that?" I asked. "There's nothing more to do?"

"Be patient. Most criminals want attention. When he feels safe enough or confident enough, he may screw up and tell someone or make some other mistake. If you want to know the truth, I think he'll do it again, and when you have two crimes to compare, you see patterns and—"

"You really think he'll kill again?"

"Not kill, unless he has to. I don't see him as a murderer so much as a sex criminal. People can kill once out of pas-sion, for instance, or maybe out of fear or desperation and never do it again; but sex criminals, those guys are almost always serial criminals. It's a compulsion. My guess is that he's done it before, and that he'll do it again."

"In the meantime, what do I do?" I asked. "Wait around for someone else to be hurt or killed?"

"It sucks, I know, but you've done all you can do."

I wasn't so sure.

For the first time in ten weeks, I put on long pants and went to work. There's always a certain apprehension about the opening of school, if only because I've been gone for so long; this was especially true in the year of Lisa Kim. I sat through two days of meetings, refusing to pay attention. I didn't want to be there. In the past, coming back had always been a transition because summer is such a pleasant distraction. Now work seemed the distraction. I felt that I should be sitting at my desk in front of my computer and lists, planning my next move. The first week of class, I took Friday off and went to Indiana to buy a gun in what was no doubt an attempt to hold off the dull, numbing sleep of winter and to prolong the electric uncertainty of that summer.

I probably could have driven there, done my business, and driven home in one day, or even stopped coming or going to the cottage, but I didn't want to. I wanted to feel comfortable there, to know my way around, to learn some street names, to walk on the sidewalks, turn the corners, so I checked into an old motel on the Red Arrow Highway Thursday evening, left Art and Cooper there with McDonald's Happy Meals, and took myself out to dinner. I didn't even hurry the next day. I took the dogs to the beach and ate a real breakfast in a real diner before I started to poke around.

I found the pawnshop first, and in it I found the gun. Then I found the church, the church custodian, and the laundromat. The church was locked, but the church custodian said there was a noon mass on Saturday and open worship until evening mass. "Then I could come in and sit quietly and pray between services?" I asked.

"That's right."

In the afternoon I used my prepaid cell phone to call the pawnshop and price the gun I had found that morning including a box of ammunition and tax. Then I went to a supermarket and purchased a cashier's check in that exact amount, using cash.

Then I found a nice pub in New Buffalo with Pilsner Urquell on tap, drank a couple pints watching the end of the Cubs game and the news, bought myself dinner again, and went back to read in bed.

The next morning, I found Alice. I also found Don, Arnelle, Cindy, and Mr. Hayes, but from the start I was pretty sure it would be Alice. Her flyer on the supermarket bulletin board was neatly handprinted and read, "House and Yard Work. Dependable Quality Cheap. No job too big. I do windows." Not one of the fringe of little tabs at the bottom had been taken. That was good. Her enterprise was new, and she was still hungry, plus she had a sense of humor. Mr. Hayes sounded old, and I liked Don, who also did yard work, but I thought I really wanted a woman; I thought I might have an emotional as well as a physical advantage if I chose a woman. Arnelle sounded okay, but Alice was my first choice, so I held my breath when I called her at two from my car.

"'Lo."

"Is this Alice?" I asked.

"Yes."

"Alice, my name is Tom. I saw your flyer in Kroger's, and I'm calling you about some work."

"You come to the right place then."

"May I ask you a few questions?"

"Course."

"Are you bonded and licensed?"

"I am not," she said without explanation or apology.

"K. How many employees do you have?"

"You talking to her. I be the CEO, CFO, and the entire rank and file, honey." She laughed easily.

"K. Please don't take this personally, but do you have a criminal record?"

"Nope. I ain't never got nothing but traffic tickets."

"No DUIs?"

"Nope."

"Are you sure about that?"

"Positive."

"Alice, do you have a car?"

"Such as it is."

"Okay, Alice." I paused for a minute, looked at my checklist, and made a decision. I told her I would like to hire her to do something other than housework. The job would take about one hour and pay three hundred dollars in cash. It would be clean, 100 percent legal, and absolutely safe. I told her I wouldn't ask her to do anything she didn't want to do, and that she could say no at any point, no questions asked, but she would have to do it right now.

"This very minute?" she asked.

"Within the next few minutes. Would you like to hear more?"

She didn't answer and I thought I'd lost her; then she said, "Keep going."

"Okay." I asked her if she knew where the church was.

"Yes, I know it." It was ten minutes from where she lived.

"Okay. If you want to take this job, go get in your car and drive to the church as soon as we hang up the phone. Go into the church—it's open—and sit in the next to the last pew on the left side. I'll come and sit in the last pew right behind you. Do not turn around. I do not want you to see me, and if you do, our deal is off. Understand?"

"What you want me to do?"

"I'll tell you when you get here. You still interested?" Again she hesitated. "Alice, if you have any qualms—"

"Honey," she said, "I can't afford me no qualms. Give me fifteen minutes." She was there in twelve. From the laundromat I watched her park her car half a block away and hurry toward the church. She was a big woman of maybe thirty-five who had bad knees and hair, but who wanted my business. Inside she was right where she was supposed to be, and I sat down behind her.

"Alice, I'm Tom. Please don't turn around."

"Uh-huh. What you want me to do?"

"Across the street there's a pawnshop called Quality Loan."

"I know it."

"If you are willing, I'll give you a money order, and you'll go to Quality Loan and purchase this item for me." I slid an index card across her shoulder and she took it.

"Item #1058. What is it?"

"It's a pistol. You ask the man for item #1058, and he'll have you fill out two forms, one state and one federal. Fill them out truthfully. As long as you're truthful, everything is perfectly legal. Then he'll make a phone call to get approval. The answer may take fifteen minutes, it may take a half hour. You either get approved, delayed, or denied. If you have no criminal record and no DUIs, you'll get approved. Then you give the man the check, and he'll give you the gun. There's an outside chance that you'll get delayed; then they have three days to approve or deny."

"Then what?"

"Then nothing. The deal's off. You come back here, sit down, I sit down behind you and give you a hundred dollars in cash for your trouble, and we say good-bye."

"That's all?"

"That's all if you can't make the purchase, but you can; you will be able to as long as you don't have a criminal record or a DUI, and it's all perfectly legal."

"Not the next part," she said.

"Hold on. You buy the gun, then come back here and sit where you are sitting. I'll sit down behind you again. You show me the item, then put it down on the pew beside you. I hand you three hundred-dollar bills." I leaned forward and fanned the bills in front of her for a moment. "You leave the item under your coat on the pew and go up to the chancel to pray . . . you Catholic?"

"For three hundred dollars I am."

"You go up to the front to pray. When you come back, the item will be gone and so will I. Then, at your convenience but within the next week—the next seven days—you go to the police and tell them exactly what happened. You bought a gun for self-protection, went to church, left it on the pew in a bundle with your coat, went to pray, and someone stole it from you. What's the world coming to. That's it. You're clear and free, and I'm long gone."

I waited.

"You sure it's legal?"

"As long as you report it."

She waited. "Listen, could I sleep on this, do it to-morrow—"

"Tomorrow's Sunday."

"Monday, then?"

"Sorry. It's a one-shot deal. It's now or never."

We both waited. She looked at the index card and read the number: "One-oh-five-eight. You got the check?" she asked me.

"I do."

She put her hand back for it. "Let's go then."

I bought a soft drink and a *Sun-Times* to occupy myself while I waited in the laundromat, but I was too nervous to even look at the paper long enough to read the headlines. I just looked out the window and at my watch. It was tak-ing forever. Maybe she had to wait for service. Maybe she called the police. No. Maybe she went out the back door with the gun. No. What was taking so long? It had been forty-two minutes. Then I turned away for a moment because a man had brought his dog into the laundromat and the Hispanic attendant was trying to get him to take it out; the man was raising his voice. I thought he might have been drinking.

I was concerned that the attendant might call the police. When I turned back, Alice was hurrying up the steps of the church; another couple of seconds, and I would have missed her. I crossed the street and stopped in the vestibule, calmed myself before stepping through the padded doors into the cool stillness of the sanctuary. I sat down and touched Alice's shoulder. She put a heavy box in a bag on her shoulder so I could see it, see the brand name and illustration, but she did not let go of it; she held it tightly. I handed her the bills, and she looked at them, rubbed them between her fingers as if they were made of fabric. Then she pulled herself heavily to her feet, saying, "Go say a prayer." She stopped, her back still to me, in the aisle. "So who am I suppose to pray for?" she asked, without expecting a reply. "I'm hoping it ain't your wife."

"Wait a minute," I said. "Don't turn around, but listen for a minute. I'm not going to shoot anyone. I'm a writer. I'm doing this for a story just to see if it can really be done. That's all."

"Uh-huh," she said. I watched her plod heavily down the aisle.

I went out the front door, down the steps, around the corner and across the one-way street, put the gun under my seat, got a single "ruff" out of Art, who was asleep, nothing out of Cooper, and drove away without passing the church again. I was on the highway in six minutes. Adrenaline made me keen. I let out a howl and a laugh that surprised myself and startled the dogs. God, I hadn't had so much fun in I didn't know how long, perhaps ever, and I told myself, "It's only a game. It's still a game." But, of course, I now owned an illegal firearm. If a cop stopped me, I would tell him just what I'd told Alice—"I'm a writer"—and driving back into the city, I thought about the story I'd already started to write.

Now I want to tell you about the day Lydia broke up with me. I've already written three versions of the story, searching, I suppose, for one in which I don't look so bad, but I can't find it. Sometimes you just look bad and there's no way around it.

It happened the next Saturday morning; it was almost as if I were the first item on her list of Saturday chores, but that's probably unfair. She did it in typical Lydia fashion: quickly, cleanly, efficiently, effectively. I would have made a mess of it, but then I didn't do it at all, did I? I guess I knew all along that if I just did nothing, Lydia would eventually do something. After all, I'd already put a deposit down on an apartment for October first and arranged to stay with John Thompson until then.

She was the first person all summer to ring my doorbell, and I had to search for the buzzer to let her in. She took one look around the apartment, at the big cluttered table, the lists on the walls, my bike, the furniture pushed back, and said, "Jesus Christ, does Carolyn know about this?"

"Don't worry; it'll all be shipshape when she gets back."

"I need to tell you something," she said still standing in the middle of the room. "I've taken a job in Milwaukee." That's how she told me that she was breaking up with me. "And I've rented a place that doesn't take pets. You're going to have to keep Art."

"Milwaukee? Is that what you were doing up there that day all dressed up?"

"Not really. It was a headhunter deal that just came out of the blue, and I did it just to see what my options were, but they ended up offering me the creative director's position, and I've taken it. So if you want, you can have the apartment. My movers are coming on Monday."

I waited. We just stood there looking at each other. "Is that it?" I said.

"Look, Pete, all summer I've been thinking about how much I love you, and I do. I know it took me a long time to admit it, and maybe that's the problem, but I do. Anyway, all summer I've been thinking about the wrong thing. I should have been thinking about how much *you* love *me,* and the answer is 'not enough.'"

"Lydia—"

She raised her hand. "Stop. It doesn't matter. All that matters now is what *I* think, and I don't think you love me. Not in the way I love you. Not in the way I need to be loved. Pete, I've lost my belief in you. You know me. I'm an extremist; I can't live on maybe and sometimes. I do not want to be lying in bed alone late at night when I'm fifty-five wondering what your latest doubt is. I can't live like that."

"Lydia—"

"No," she said. "The thing is broken irreparably. It can't be fixed; it won't heal. I know that I can never trust you again, not with my heart. I tried all summer to get you to love me, and now the summer is over. Now I'm going to leave, and I'm going to ask you to let me. All your attempts to be a nice guy have only made things worse, so please let me go." She stood up and looked at me. She went out the door. I watched her go down the stairs. Then I went to the window and watched her cross the street.

———

I had no intention of killing the doctor. None at all. It was research or a game or a great indulgence, a return to the summers of my youth. Now I was pretending again, pretending to be a detective or a mystery novelist or the right hand of God. And I was having an enormous amount of fun. Still, I know that the only difference between a passenger and a skydiver is a single step, and the closer I got to the open hatch, the more exciting and pregnant my fantasy became. And I must admit that somewhere in me I knew that the ultimate thrill would be to discover that it wasn't a fantasy at all.

That's why I took the bullet that night. I had never intended to, but at the last minute I knew that it just wouldn't be the same with an empty pistol. I wanted verisimilitude. I wanted to feel that adrenaline rush again. I wanted to have the doctor in my sights and to make the decision not to pull the trigger. And I thought that I had everything planned right down to the last second and the final detail, but as it turned out, I was in no way prepared for what happened.

I practically idled up Sheridan Road refusing to even think about my destination, a man in search of a lake breeze on a warm autumn evening listening to a ball game on the radio. The Cubs were playing out the string and the announcers were working very hard—too hard—to not sound bored silly, distracted, and tired of it all.

I parked at the far end of the lot with a clear view of the doctor's black BMW. I opened the *Trib* over the steering wheel, section by section, and slowly the lot began to empty. When the spot to the left of the doctor's car became available, I looked at it a long time and then idled forward into it. This upped the stakes. Now I not only had means and motive, I had opportunity. I had proximity. In a few minutes he would be practically close enough to touch, certainly close enough to kill. My heart beat in my ears.

But it wasn't a few minutes. It was forty-five minutes after his last appointment had ended. It was getting dark and there were just three cars parked in the lot now, all side by side, with the doctor's in the middle. As each faded ray of light made my enterprise more conceivable, more possible, I imagined the scene. I envisioned it. I picked the heavy, cool gun up, held it, raised it to the open passenger window of my car. Too close, I thought. He would be right there. How could I shoot something—someone—so close? Blood would splatter. It might splatter on me. He might fall against my car and smear blood on it. I saw myself driving back down the lakeshore with a big smear of human blood on my passenger door, specks of blood on my glasses. What if he fell under my car, fell and rolled under my wheels? Drive over him? Get out and pull him away by the feet? I had almost come to the conclusion that I couldn't shoot him, that I couldn't shoot anything at such horrifyingly, intimately close range. But of course that would be the exact time to do it; when you thought you couldn't possibly, when you were absolutely sure you wouldn't. Then blam! And "intimate" was the word. It would be a very intimate act; I had not realized that. It would be as intimate as kissing him, as intimate—more intimate— than sex. . . .

I heard voices. He wasn't alone. "Shit," I said, relieved. I saw two figures cross my rearview mirror: a man and a woman. Quickly the doctor was at the door of his car and across my car I could see his torso. I held my breath. I had never been this close to him. Then the woman was there, too. She touched his elbow and pressed against him.

"Don't" he said. "We can't." Then she disappeared, and just as quickly, he had closed his door and started his engine and backed away like a drawn curtain, and there was the woman unlocking her car door and getting in.

"Oh fuck," I said. It was Tanya Kim. She heard me. She looked toward me. She backed out and was gone into the night.

Lydia left me a rug, a dresser, a coatrack, a boom box, a coffee table, an easy chair, most of the dishes, flatware, pots and pans, and an old-but-good maple dining-room set with ladder-back chairs that had once belonged to my parents. I instantly transferred my operation to this table and taped my lists around it, although by the middle of October, the lists were mostly new. I bought a bed, borrowed a couple of lamps, and brought home one of the couches students had donated to my classroom. For the time being, I didn't buy a television. I like TV, but I didn't have any time for it that fall; I was too busy. Unfortunately, what I was busy with was very seldom schoolwork, so in early November, I went to see John Thompson and told him that I needed some time off. I told him I wanted to take a leave of absence. He listened to my plans.

"How much time do you want?" he asked.

"One year, two semesters."

"If you do this, will you come all the way back and be the teacher you used to be?"

"Yes. I will or I'll resign."

He looked at me, thinking. "Tell you what I want you to do," he said. "Go home and write a letter of application to the sabbatical committee. Tell them you want to do some writing; you've got the credentials for that. You're way past the deadline, but who knows. Can't hurt to try, and you might get half your salary."

I invited Tanya Kim to dinner at my apartment three weeks before Christmas. I was straight with her on the phone; I told her I had things to tell her about Lisa and Decarre. I did not tell her that I had also invited Decarre's other two victims, Dorothy Murrell and Jeanette Landrow, nor at the last minute, Carolyn O'Connor, thinking that the others might feel more comfortable with another woman there. Carolyn could put anyone at her ease.

I decided to make a casserole, a favorite of mine with hot Italian sausage, artichoke hearts, rice, green peas, and Parmesan cheese. More of a man's dish, I suppose, but mighty good on a chilly, winter evening, and I'd serve it with a big mesclun salad full of nuts, berries and cherry tomatoes and good, crusty bread. I had tiny lemon tarts as a sweet, and three cheeses with fruit for afterwards.

About mid-afternoon it began to snow, and I thought for sure someone would use that as an excuse, someone wouldn't show, but they all did. Carolyn was the first to arrive. She brought some red-pepper hummus and her pictures of Europe, but I was too busy and nervous to look at them. "Hey," she said when she saw my Trek. "That's a serious bike."

"Pretty, isn't it?"

"I thought you were the guy who said you could find

everything you needed in life at a garage sale. I don't think you got that at a garage sale."

"No, I sold out. I even got a helmet and a spandex outfit."

Jeanette came next. She carried with her a file that she held against her chest even after she was also holding a glass of red wine. She leaned against the kitchen counter, and we spoke of Christmas plans as I prepared dinner. Then came Dorothy. She was nervous and laughed a lot. Jeanette and Dorothy shyly, curiously, looked at each other when they had a chance, when the other was saying something. When the chatter died for a moment, Jeanette said, "I guess it's kind of an intervention, isn't it?"

Tanya came last. I poured her a glass of wine and carried a plate of crackers and hummus out to the living room, then went back to the kitchen and turned up the music. I realized then that I could feel my heart beating, and I raised my eyebrows at Carolyn and said, "We'll see." I half-expected Tanya to be gone when we went into the living room, or maybe all of them to be gone, but they weren't. Instead they were all sitting on the couch with Tanya in the middle. The two other women were doing the talking and mostly to each other, but Tanya was listening. She was listening and watching. The talk went on at dinner, and at times it gushed out, as if in relief. Everyone relaxed. Carolyn and I just listened, but we were not excluded. It was as if all of us were a part of a secret club, and I guess we were.

Tanya didn't say much, and she didn't show much, but she did drink a lot of wine and in the end both Carolyn and Dorothy offered to drop her off, but she said no, she wasn't driving; she wanted to walk.

At the door I said to Carolyn, "I never looked at the pictures."

"We could now quickly."

"I don't want to do it quickly, and I'm too pooped anyway. Let's have dinner next week, and I'll see them then."

"Okay, sure," she said. "Call me."

"Thanks for tonight," I said.

At midnight, as I was finishing the dishes, I thought to myself that neither Tanya nor I had acknowledged that it was the anniversary of Lisa Kim's death, and I wondered if Tanya even realized it.

On Monday I got a letter with Mexican postage on it. It was addressed to both Lydia and me, and that made me feel for just a second as if I'd gone over a rise in a fast car. I hadn't bothered to tell Charlie, and I imagined that Lydia hadn't, either.

Charlie's Christmas letters were famous between Lydia and me. They consisted of his usual picturesque prose decorated with winking lights and sparkling bulbs. I made a cup of tea to enjoy with it, then sat down at my big table and opened it.

Dear Pete and Lydia,

I'm very sorry to have to inform you that Charlie died of a heart attack in October after he had gone back to school. He had a slight attack teaching and was immediately taken to the hospital. I talked to him by phone that evening, and we made plans for my coming to drive him home in a couple of days.

That night, however, he suffered another attack that
was massive and fatal. He was in intensive care and
surrounded by doctors, but they could not save him.

Since then I've been busy with his affairs. Two of
his children were down for a memorial service.
He was cremated and buried here at the ranch.

Charlie was a man with many friends, and
he counted you among the best of them. I'm
sure you'll keep him in kind memory.

Sincerely,

Dick

There's a painting by John Sloan in the Art Institute of Chicago called *Renganeschi's Saturday Night,* that shows three young women out to dinner in a popular New York restaurant in 1912. The tablecloths are white, the waiters tuxedoed and the place is busy, crowded, and gay. The painting always reminds me of Mia Francesca, the spot Carolyn and I had dinner that Friday night. It's a narrow, bright, loud, and festive room on North Clark Street, just around the corner from Carolyn's place. She already had a table against the wall and a glass of red wine when I came in.

"Thought I better get a place. It fills up fast."

"I'll have whatever she's drinking," I said. "Cold out." We talked about the cold and Christmas and Carolyn's new job and Tanya Kim, who had left me a thank-you phone message and said she was going to send me something that hadn't arrived yet. We talked about that evening.

"You know, it was really interesting," Carolyn said. "These three women . . . they couldn't decide if they were rivals or allies. I've never felt a stranger dynamic in a room, yet it wasn't bad. It was good, really. Don't you think it turned out well?"

"I'm just glad it's over." I thanked her for recommending Gene, and we talked about him. She said she liked that he didn't make judgments rashly.

I said, "Neither do you, you know. I don't know if you've always been like that or if you learned it from Gene, but it seems to me you've always been like that. When people were rolling their eyes behind my back, you treated me as if I might actually be sane. I mean, I did go a little overboard there for a while."

"Maybe, but when you told us about the accident, I was touched. I think it was because you believed that you could have done something—very few people think that they can—and maybe even more, that you should have done something—even fewer of us think that—and I guess I liked that you believed in yourself when you must have known that other people were doubting you, so I just kind of decided to believe in you, too, and it turns out that your instincts were pretty good and I guess mine were, too."

"Then you don't think what I'm going to do is hare-brained?" I asked.

"I think it's what you need to do."

"Think it will work?"

"Who knows, Pete. I have no idea. What are we toasting?"

"I'm saying good-bye."

"Good-bye?"

"I'm going to Mexico." Carolyn raised her eyebrows. "It's

cheap and I'm not going to have a lot of money. And I really like Mexico; I feel at home there, and I figure I can make a little money writing travel pieces."

"To Mexico, then." She raised her wineglass.

I looked at her and she at me and we smiled. "I did fall a little bit in love with her, you know."

"I know."

"I think its time to get beyond that, too. I've been thinking I might start dating again."

"Good. I think you're ready for that," she said.

"Yeah, but I don't know where to begin."

"You must know a lot of eligible women. Aren't schools full of them?"

"Yeah, but I'm not sure I want to date someone I work with. And I'm not sure . . . that's the thing. What am I looking for? I don't want to do this the same way I did it when I was twenty-two, and you can imagine what criteria I used then. No, I said to myself, don't even think about sex or love or romance or marriage. Think about one thing: Think about someone you would really enjoy having dinner with, nothing more. So I decided to make a list. I went to Café Express with a pad and pen and I wrote down your name, naturally, since we do this from time to time, and I always enjoy it, and then I couldn't think of anyone else whom I'd rather have dinner with, or even whom I'd like to have dinner with, so I stopped."

She looked at me strangely. "What are you saying?"

"I'm saying that I'd like to write you while I'm away. May I do that?"

She didn't answer. She was flustered, and I liked that she

hadn't seen it coming. For all her wisdom and intelligence, there was something in her that was also naïve and innocent. She regained her composure as we looked at the photographs, ate our meals, and talked of other people. Steve's doing this, Wendy's doing that, and someone else something else. She asked if I had talked to Lydia.

"No. You?"

"We haven't talked." She had called and left two or three messages, but Lydia hadn't called back, and Carolyn thought that meant that she wasn't interested in continuing their friendship. Too many associations, probably. By this time we had paid our bill and were standing in front of the restaurant on the pavement, and Carolyn asked me where I was parked.

"I'm right on your block. Can I walk you home?"

"Sure." I think we were both trying not to touch each other—not even to brush shoulders—but when we came to an icy patch, I took her elbow, and when we got to her steps, she asked me if I wanted to walk Cooper with her.

"Sure." Cooper was happy to see me. We followed him down to Halsted Street and back to Clark Street, and when we got there, Carolyn said, "I'll buy you a nightcap at The Outpost."

"What about Cooper?"

"We'll tie him to the no-parking sign, and everyone who comes by will pet him. He'll love it." So we sat at the bar sipping Grand Marnier and watching Cooper through the plate-glass window. Carolyn mused, then turned to me and said, "Pete, I know we've known each other a long time, but I still don't think you know me very well."

"I know you have strong friendships," I said. "I know you like to travel and scuba dive. I know your favorite color is green. I know you don't allow dogs on your furniture. I know you love to read."

"Reading is almost my favorite thing to do."

"And cooking," I said, "and singing."

"Yes," but she said she sang only in big groups or entirely alone. She wanted me to know that; she didn't like to stand out; she didn't like to be the life of the party. "I can't tell a joke, and public speaking gives me panic attacks."

"Not good for a lawyer."

"That's why I'm not a litigator. I do not like to be the center of attention. It makes me nervous. I do not like the limelight. A lot of people find me a little boring."

"I do not, and you still haven't told me anything I don't know. Tell me something that will surprise me."

"I'm a nervous driver. I'm scared of heights. I hate football."

"I'm still not surprised."

"Okay, I don't like Christmas very much except for the music and I hate 'Little Drummer Boy.' "

"Something more."

"You have a white car and I don't like white cars."

"What's wrong with 'Little Drummer Boy'?"

"It's repetitive and sentimental."

"Why don't you like Christmas?"

"It's a hard day for single people. I always try to be traveling on Christmas Day."

"And white cars?"

"They look like kitchen appliances."

I held up my glass. "Would you like another one of these?"

"And I never have more than one nightcap. See, I'm a real stick-in-the-mud."

We walked back. She was standing at the top of the steps with Cooper about to open the door, and I was standing at the bottom when I called her name. "Carolyn."

"Yes?"

"May I write you?"

She thought about that for a moment. "Yes," she said.

BOOK TWO
. . .

SOME TIME LATER, WITH A CONTEMPORARY INTERLUDE

1

• • •

TRAVEL WRITING

DATELINE: SAN MIGUEL DE ALLENDE, MEXICO
by Pete Ferry

I T WAS LYDIA's first time in Mexico. We were quite young. My Spanish was a bit rusty, and she didn't speak any yet. I had just gotten my first travel-writing assignments, and I was anxious to get going, but all Lydia wanted to do was hang around San Miguel de Allende.

Not that there is anything wrong with San Miguel de Allende. It is a lovely place, really, one of a handful of towns scattered across Mexico that have been declared national monuments in their entireties and preserved because of their colonial character. That means a cathedral, narrow cobblestone streets, plazas and bandstands, arcades and tile roofs, a colorful town market, adobe walls over which orange and bright purple bougainvilleas crawl and drape, and tantalizing glimpses from the street through a door just closing or one left ajar of private inner spaces, of courtyards, fountains, flowers, secret trees, and hanging baskets of green, blue, and yellow birds.

Maybe it is because San Miguel is so lovely a place or that it has an excellent art school and a couple of little language schools that there are just a few too many Americans around. Enough so that the waiters all speak English, that there's an English-language bookstore on the main plaza, a good pizza place one block from it and, depressingly, a subdivision just outside of town that is occupied almost exclusively by retired gringos.

Of course, as a first timer, it was all of this minus the sub-division that Lydia liked, but as a "professional travel writer," it was all of this especially the subdivision that I found embarrassing. I wanted to go somewhere where I could use my bad Spanish and good phrase-book, where they didn't have Cobb salad on every menu, and where they didn't take American Express. Instead we ate at Mama Mia's three nights running because the pizza was good and also cheap, which I used as a justification because neither of us had much money. Besides, we liked the waitstaff, which was young, casual, irreverent, and after nine there was live music on the tiny stage in the open courtyard. But three nights was enough. I wanted to leave the next day. Lydia wanted to stay through the weekend to see the guitarist we saw the first night. We quarreled and compromised; we'd stay Friday night and leave early Saturday morning.

In the meantime I spent a day driving over the mountain to visit Guanajuato, the old silver-mining capital of the region full of stately nineteenth-century government and university buildings and built quite dramatically in a narrow, winding canyon. I saw no other Americans, spoke Spanish all day long, and drove home feeling mollified and self-righteous.

Strangely, Lydia felt exactly the same; she had explored the part of San Miguel on the hillside above the center and found the little bullring I had searched for in vain, then spent the afternoon in the studios of the Instituto Allende chatting with other painters. We were each a little smug over our pizza that night, and I think we were both wondering just how much we needed each other. The courtyard at Mama Mia's began to fill up, and we turned our chairs toward the stage. Just before nine, five Mexican men crowded into the table next to us. One of them was a big guy with broad shoulders, a bushy mustache, and a big white smile. They talked in loud Spanish. They were wearing cowboy hats and boots, new blue jeans, and brightly colored shirts with snaps rather than buttons. They seemed like farmers out on the town, but they had more money than I expected farmers to have, and they were out of place in a crowd of tourists and urban Mexicans. The big guy stepped on Lydia's foot coming back to the table and apologized in English. She made her stock joke about having two of them, and he laughed appreciatively.

The guitarist came out and then a singer. She was the reason for the crowd; she was very good and sang love songs and ballads in both Spanish and English. A few people got up to slow-dance. We were delivered a pitcher of sangria compliments, it turns out, of the big guy. I guessed that was where he went. This was all quite awkward because he wasn't sitting across the room, but immediately beside us, and there was nothing to do but grin, nod, clink glasses and toast each other. Still, we'd already had a few drinks, drinking at six thousand feet is problematic to begin with, and Lydia seemed a bit tipsy. I tried to catch her eye, but couldn't. Then when the musicians took a break, the Mexicans engaged us. Where were we from? What were we doing in central Mexico? Did we like it here?

Lydia was in her element, and I had fun watching her. She had a brand of gay repartee and easy banter tailor-made for this situation. Pretty soon she had all five laughing, even the two who clearly didn't speak much English. I was now aware of a little guy in addition to the big guy. He may have been the big guy's sidekick or it may have been the other way around. At any rate, they were a tag team; they had lots of eye contact, sidebars, and inside jokes.

There was more music, and at the next break I offered to share the pitcher of sangria the big guy bought us and was relieved when the Mexicans accepted; but when I came back from the bathroom, there was another pitcher on the table, and when I tried to beg off using the elevation as a reason, I saw the big guy's eyes were not on me but on Lydia's face next to me, and out of the corner of my eye I saw that she was mouthing something to him. Okay, I got it. There had clearly been a conversation in my absence, and I was now an unwitting player in one of the pocket dramas Lydia regularly produced. This one was called "Pete the prig vs. Lydia the free spirit," and I knew the only way out of it was not to get in it, so I shut up, but it may already have been too late. Then a little later I heard the big guy say to the little guy, *"No lleva sostén."* She's not wearing a bra.

The little guy answered, *"Tal vez tampoco lleva las bragas."* Maybe she's not wearing panties, either.

I said, *"Las lleva."* Yes, she is. Then in English I said, "I watched her put them on," and smiled.

There was an awkward silence. Then the big guy laughed loudly and slapped my back. "You speak Spanish, my friend!"

"Un poco."

"Please do not take offense. It is just that your wife is a very pretty girl."

"She's not my wife," I said.

"Then your fiancée . . ."

"She's not that, either."

"Your friend?" asked the little guy.

"I guess we haven't figured out what we are. We're working on that. Right now we're just traveling companions."

"Then you won't mind if I ask her to dance?" asked the big guy.

"Of course not."

He enfolded her in his arms. He was very large and she was very small. Back at the tables (they had been pushed together), he talked earnestly to her about something while tapping her forearm with his very large index finger. The little guy was sitting on the other side of Lydia, his arm draped across the back of her chair. I leaned over and whispered in her ear, "Have you ever gone to bed with a Mexican?"

She laughed. "Not yet."

"Have you ever gone to bed with five?" I asked.

She laughed again. "Oh stop it!"

I gave up. I turned back to the stage. There was more music, more wine, more dancing. Things got a little blurred for me. Then the guitarist was putting his instrument back in its case, the waiters were putting chairs up on the tables, and the little guy had sat down beside me to say, "My friend, we would like you and Lydia to be our guests. There is a wonderful cantina outside of town—"

"What's it called?" I asked.

"It's called La Casa del Fuego. . . ."

"It's a brothel," I said. "I read about it."

He dipped his head once. "There are women there, yes, but it is many things. It is also a restaurant and a nightclub and a casino, and it's open all night."

"No, thank you. We have to get an early start tomorrow."

"Oh come on." Lydia was suddenly sitting where the little man had been. "This sounds like fun."

"You promised," I said. "It's already one o'clock and I want to be in Oaxaca by tomorrow night."

"Come on, Pete, we're on vacation."

"No," I said firmly. "I'm not getting in a car with a bunch of drunken Mexicans I don't know."

"Is that it? Is it that they're Mexicans?"

"Of course not."

"Then why did you say that?" Now we were standing on the sidewalk in front of Mama Mia's and the Mexicans were waiting for us down the block.

"Because we're in Mexico, for Chrissake. If we were in Albania, I'd have said 'Albanians.'" I knew that sounded bad as soon as I said it.

"And if we were in Columbus, you'd say 'drunken Ohioans'?" She was laughing at me. "Sure you would." She turned away.

"Lydia, where are you going?"

"I told you; I wanna see this cantina. I'm going with them."

I caught her elbow. "I can't let you do that." At that elevation, at that hour, at that level of inebriation, it was the wrong thing to say, and I knew it.

"You what?"

"Nothing."

"You can't let me do it? You can't stop me from doing it. Watch." She turned and walked loosely if unsteadily toward the men. One of them was watching her breasts. She hooked her arms through two of theirs, and they all went down the middle of the street and got into a big white pickup truck. Its lights came on, and it drove away from me. I could hear ranchero music blasting from it. The truck went around a turnabout and came back toward me, the music filling the empty street. Three of the men stood in the bed leaning on the cab. I could see the little guy was driving and I could see the big guy was riding shotgun. As the truck passed me picking up speed, I could see Lydia sitting between them, her small, round, alabaster face lighted momentarily by the streetlight, her eyes fixed straight ahead.

2

. . .

THE DOCTOR

REALIZED ONE summer day that I was spending entirely too much time sitting at my desk by the window
in my room, and I got up early to cross the plaza with
Art and eat a good breakfast in the sidewalk café beneath the
arcades. I even bought the English-language paper, hoping
to find out how the Cubs were doing. In it beneath a heading that read, "Whereabouts—Please contact the American
Embassy," halfway down a long list of names, I found mine.
It surprised me. Was I missing? I tried to remember the last
time I had talked to or even written anyone at home except
Carolyn; it seemed as if it had been days, but it had been
weeks, many weeks. Actually, I hadn't called home since I'd
left San Miguel and come here. Later I put some pesos in the
beggar's tin.

The beggar had a lot to do with why I didn't leave my
room often: the beggar, the fruit cart, and my work. Despite

the steepness of the hill, the stones in the street were so large
and irregular that there was little danger of the fruit cart rolling away. The beggar sat behind the fruit cart in the shelter
of a doorway with a rusted sardine tin beside him. He looked
like a pile of refuse that the street sweeper was sure to come
back for. The only part of his anatomy that you could pick out
from his colorless heap was his face, featureless and organ-
less now, looking like a swollen, misshapen fist. When you
dropped a coin into the tin, the beggar scrambled to recover
it and then waved it impatiently, almost frantically, above his
head until the fruit-cart man came to replace it with a banana, an orange, a slice of melon, a few nuts, a mango, a piece
of papaya, a tangerine or a slice of coconut with a streak of
hot sauce across it. The beggar ate with the same impatience,
clutching and gulping his each morsel like a chipmunk, and
when it was gone, waited for more footsteps, another coin,
more food. I didn't like the beggar much, but he fascinated
me. I didn't even pity him because he was just too far removed from the whole of my experience, but I had come to
realize lately I envied him a little. I'd been tempted several
times to drop a few hundred pesos in that tin of his and watch
the fruit-cart man dump his entire inventory on the beggar's
head. Perhaps it was his table manners that offended me so.

Late in the day after the rain, the high-plateau sun beyond
my roof shined down into the street onto the fruit cart and
reduced everything for a few minutes to color, a few colors,
insistent primary colors like a child's finger painting. Early
in the morning before the beggar came, even before the fruit
cart came, a woman carrying a pan of water opened a door

in the wall and washed yesterday's peels and rinds and shells into the gutter.

We all need our monsters—that much is certain—and sometimes they need each other; neither Saddam Hussein nor George Bush was very interesting all alone. The same is true of Mr. Claggart and Billy Budd, or should that pairing be Mr. Claggart and Captain Vere? I think so. As for everyone's favorite monster, Adolf Hitler's greatest contribution to destruction in our time wasn't a worldwide war or the murder of twelve million, but providing the rest of us with a model of absolute evil just when we had wisely begun to doubt its existence. Since 1945, God only knows how many lives have been given and taken in the name of morality; certainly righteousness is the greatest destructive force on the planet today.

I saw Albert Decarre six times as a patient in the months after I got home from Mexico, though I'd intended to see him only once. The first time I told him I was haunted by something that I had seen and something that I knew, but we didn't discuss either of those things until the last time I saw him. What we did talk about was my family, the love my parents shared for forty-one years, and the guilt I felt for hurting Lydia.

"Can you tell me about that relationship?"

I told him that it had everything a relationship is supposed to have except something neither of us was ever quite able to define, but both of us knew was missing.

He took notes. "The thing that was missing. Did you see it in your parents' relationship?"

"I suppose. I think it was like glue, something that bonded them, some absolute commitment, the 'in sickness and health, for richer for poorer, for better for worse' part. That wasn't there. I always knew that something would happen, and we wouldn't be strong enough to survive it, and we'd come apart. And we did."

I should tell you that despite myself, I liked Albert Decarre. He was intelligent, empathetic, thoughtful, helpful, troubled, and world-weary. His face was deeply lined and his eyes sunken, things that had not shown up in his photograph. He carried sadness with him. He was also quite elegant; that's the only word for it. He was slim, graceful, and soft-spoken. His clothes fit perfectly. His hair fell just so. At the same time, he always seemed to be on the very verge of something you didn't want to be the cause of. Within minutes of meeting him, I knew exactly why Jeanette Landrow had been afraid of hurting him.

My sessions with Albert Decarre were really conversations; if he was thoughtful and soft-spoken, he was not reticent. He listened well but he also spoke well, and we often built on each other's ideas, and we sometimes came to important conclusions. This happened at least twice.

But if I liked Albert Decarre in the beginning, I did not trust him. I knew as well as anyone that Lucifer can be beguiling. I never forgot that his ease, charm, and apparent confidentiality (he could be surprisingly forthcoming) were all tricks that had seduced others and could seduce me, too. I came to realize, however, that there was a difference between them and me: If he was tricking me, I was also tricking him. Sometimes I sat there watching him as he recrossed his legs and talked, or absentmindedly stroked his chin and talked, and I would have to repress a smile; I was the safe that was about to fall on his head, the car that was about to veer across the centerline into his lane. There were even times when the satisfaction I felt was tinged with some feeling for him; I was, after all, going to destroy him, and anyone—even a bad man—who is about to meet his fate can enlist our sympathy. I came to think of this as a twist on the Stockholm syndrome; I was the captor and I was beginning to identify with him, the captive; of course, he didn't know he was a captive at all. Later my identification would become different and stronger.

Most of the conversations we had were about love, the nature of love. One of the important conclusions we reached— and I think it fair to say we reached it together—was that just because one doesn't love another anymore doesn't mean that he or she never did, that the death of love is as natural a phenomenon as the birth or existence of love, and that love doesn't have to commit suicide or be murdered; it can die naturally, accidentally or even incidentally. It can die even when we don't want it to, just like a person. I was naturally thinking of Lydia, Lisa, and Carolyn when we talked about this stuff. As I watched Decarre, I wondered who he was thinking of.

Another thing Decarre said that I tried to apply to both of us was, "The hardest truth of all is that sometimes in this life you must hurt other people. Not that you do or can, but that you must." He compared these occasions on a personal level to earthquakes, forest fires, and natural selection on a global one. He said that they are necessary—if painful—adjustments for the greater good and to avoid them is to invite

264 ... PETER FERRY

imbalance and worse. It may surprise you to know that as he said these things, I didn't sense that he was justifying or rationalizing, so much as realizing. Naturally I thought about myself and Lydia, and I thought about Albert and Lisa, and then I thought about him and me. And that is when my identification with him truly crystallized because I suddenly knew that I had to do what I was about to do, exactly because he had had to do what he had done. Any doubt I may have had was erased. He and I were alike; we were both beset by lamentable compulsion. I scheduled my final session with him and left.

One week minus one hour later, I put my backpack with its precious cargo on the floor and settled into the now-familiar chair. Albert Decarre sat across the coffee table. I told him I thought it was time to talk about the thing I had seen and the thing I knew. He asked me what I had seen.

"I saw someone die."

"Um," he said, "I'm sorry. That can be very hard. Did you know the person who died?"

"Not beforehand, but I got to know her afterward."

"After her death?"

"Yes. In fact I quite fell in love with her."

"After she was dead?" he asked.

"Yes," I said. "Actually the only time I ever saw her was on the occasion of her death."

"May I ask you how she died?"

"It was an accident. At least it seemed so at the time."

"And you saw it happen?"

"I saw the whole thing."

"I want to ask you something else. Did you cause the accident?"

"No."

"Did you have anything to do with her death?"

"No, except I think—or I thought for a long time—that I could have prevented it."

"You no longer think that?"

"No, I don't think so. Not very often."

"So you have some doubt?"

"A little."

He took some notes and I watched him. He had an unusually expressive mouth. He had long white fingers. He crossed his legs in that way that thin people can so that the one fairly dangled from the other. "A while ago, you said that something happened that your relationship with Lydia wouldn't be able to survive. Is this what happened?"

"Yes."

"And you fell in love with the woman who died?"

"Yes, I fell in love with her. The other shoe dropped."

"Interesting phrase. Do you often feel that the other shoe's about to drop?"

"No, I don't think so, but I did in that relationship."

"Do you feel that now?"

"Now? I guess I do, in a way, but in a very different way. More as in 'resolution,' and I guess that's why I've come to see you."

He turned back a page. "Resolution of what's been haunting you?"

"In a way."

"Tell me this," he said. "Do you think you could ever have the kind of relationship with a woman that your parents had?"

"Well, I hope so. I think that's what we're all looking for, don't you?"

The doctor ignored my question. He said that he dealt with a lot of people who've had inadequate models in their lives, or bad models, but sometimes having a good model—a model that's too good—is the hardest thing of all. He called it the famous-parent syndrome. If a parent has been extremely successful, it's a hard thing for a child to live up to. He can never make as much money, build as big a house, write as good a book, hit as many home runs as his father, and even if he does then he knows people will say, "Well, it was just because of his dad. His father made it possible."

"You think my parents' marriage was too ideal, and I can never live up to it?" I asked

"It's possible. One thing that interests me is that you chose to fall in love with someone who was unattainable."

"I didn't exactly choose her," I said.

"You fell in love with someone unattainable. There is no one less attainable than a dead person, and you may be surprised to know that lots of people fall in love with dead people." He smiled. "It's another syndrome." He called it the widow's syndrome. A man dies after a difficult or troubled marriage, and his wife turns him into a saint, forgets the dirty socks on the floor, the drinking, or the womanizing, and romanticizes him, turns him into the husband she'd always wanted, and ends up loving him more in death than she ever did in life.

"And you think that's what I'm doing?" I asked.

"It's possible," said the doctor. "You see, loving someone who isn't there is safer than loving someone who is, which is why 'absence makes the heart grow fonder.' There's no more profound absence than death, and when someone's dead, you can make her anyone you want her to be."

"I don't know. It seems a little pat."

"Okay, tell me more. Why do you think you fell in love with this dead woman?"

I told him that guilt was a factor, that she was beautiful and interesting and vulnerable.

"Vulnerable after her death?" he asked.

"In an odd way. I told you I saw something and I know something. That has to do with what I know."

"And what is that?"

"I know that her death wasn't really an accident, or at least it was an intentional accident."

"An accident she intended? Did she commit suicide?"

"No. She was killed."

"Oh. Murdered?" he asked.

"Yes, she was murdered, and I know who did it."

"How do you know this?" he asked.

"I saw the man who did it."

"You saw him do it? You saw him kill her?"

"No, but I saw him, and I know he did it. I put two and two together, and I know."

"Pete, may I ask you what your purpose is with regard to this man?"

"I would like to see him brought to justice, of course."

"May I ask then why you don't just go to the police?"

"I did. That's one of the first things I did." I waited and watched him.

"And were they able to help you?"

I told him that they helped me see that I knew nothing about police work, that my "case" against the man was intuitive, my evidence was either missing or circumstantial, that the man was a highly respected citizen with no criminal record, and that I appeared to be on either a wild-goose chase or a crusade. Here are the things I did not tell him: "They" was Steve Lotts, who now believed the man to be involved in the woman's death, Lieutenant Grassi may have suspected foul play early on, and I now had a lot more evidence that I hadn't taken to the police because I wanted to be able to act if they did not. "They said that no prosecutor would dare to touch the thing, and if one did, he'd get laughed out of the DA's office. They suggested I seek counseling."

"Okay."

"So here I am. Seeking counseling."

"All right. How are you feeling about all of this now?"

"What do you mean?"

"I presume since you came 'seeking resolution,' that you are not finished with it quite yet."

"No, no. They did make me step back and take a closer, more realistic look at myself and my motives and the whole situation. I mean, why was I doing this? What did it really matter to me?" I told him that I no longer saw the woman as a purely innocent victim; she was too complex for that. For that matter, I no longer saw the man as completely evil. I didn't like what he did, but I began to understand it at least a little; I could at least imagine his desperation. I mentioned for the first time that the man was a doctor, that the woman was his patient, that they were having an affair, and that I was quite certain now that at least on some level—if only the emotional one—she was blackmailing him. She was getting to him somehow, that he was an essentially good man who made one mistake and was in danger of being destroyed by it. He was a modest, intelligent, circumspect man about to become a tabloid headline, a man who had devoted his life to helping others undone by the most human of desires, a man trapped perhaps (who knows?) in a loveless marriage, a cold, difficult wife, a lonely man empty, aging, and then this woman—this young woman—this beautiful, vital, exciting, sexy, daring, tempting, willing, able, very able, very willing, and very vulnerable girl came along, and of course it went sour, and she turned into a viper, and he was faced with utter ruin. I told him that I thought a lot about the despair, desperation, and panic the doctor must have felt, about the scandal, the shame and disgrace that he knew lay ahead of him, about that Noah Cross line in *Chinatown:* "Most people never have to face the fact that at the right time, at the right place, they're capable of anything." I even told him that I thought of some of the things I'd been capable of and some of the things I'd done that I regret. I told him I'd done things I wished I hadn't. I looked at him.

"Do you want to tell me about those things?" he asked.

"No, not really. Not now, anyway. See, I needed to resolve this thing about the doctor. I came to realize my fallacy was my starting point; he's not an essentially good man; he just looks like one. Look closer and you see a physician who betrayed his most essential trust, who hurt a patient who came to him for help, who hurt her premeditatedly, repeatedly, perhaps as an act of passion originally, but later dispassionately, and when he feared getting caught, he abandoned her. Abandoned her as a lover, as a human being, as a patient. And when she struck back, he killed her."

"Hm."

"There's more. There's the man in the camel coat and the woman who might have been his wife. See, we met at the wreck. They were driving north as I was driving south. Had the young woman swerved left rather than going straight into the tree, she might have hit them. Of course, the woman who might have been his wife might *not* have been his wife, and for all I know, he was about to hit her over the head or dump her in the lake or she him, all of which is to say that I'm really not much of a sentimentalist myself, but you'd have to consider who else you might be endangering, wouldn't you?" I looked at him carefully and closely.

"So where does that leave you?" he finally asked.

"You mean in the 'is the doctor good or is the doctor evil' thing?"

"If you wish." And I thought for an instant that he was genuinely interested in my answer.

"My guess used to be neither," I said. "My guess used to be that he was more amoral than immoral, that he was something of a sociopath. That he really had no feelings. That he could probably have sat right here and discussed this thing coolly and objectively without raising his blood pressure or breaking a sweat. He could probably have even passed a polygraph test if it was in his own interest to do so. That's what I used to feel. Now I'm not so sure."

"Do you think it would make you feel better if you were able to punish him?" he asked.

"That's not it, you see. I don't want to punish him, I just want to stop him."

"Then you feel you have a moral purpose?"

"I came to feel that he was a man without one." I looked him in the eyes as I explained that the doctor had crossed a line a doctor just can't cross, not once or ever. And if he ever did, he'd misunderstood the basic relationship between doctor and patient, that there isn't any margin for error. This wasn't an error. This wasn't a slipup or mistake. It was fundamental betrayal. And if a doctor does it once, he's probably done it before, and he'll probably do it again.

"So you felt you needed to stop him. . . ."

"No. Not without more evidence. So, you know what I did?" I had run an ad in the *Evanston Review,* the *Wilmette Life,* all the little papers on the North Shore headed "Ph. D. Study of Clinical Abuse." It read: "I am writing my dissertation on clinical psychiatrists, psychologists, and social workers who take sexual, psychological, or emotional advantage of their patients. If you would like to be part of the study, please contact me through P.O. box such-and-such, confidentiality guaranteed." When I told Decarre this, he uncrossed and recrossed his legs. He worked hard not to take his eyes off mine, and succeeded. "Got some very interesting replies," I said. "Fewer than you'd think, or fewer than a layman might think, I guess. Funny how we are suspicious of head doctors like we are of lawyers. Maybe not. Anyway, I interviewed them all. Most you could dismiss almost immediately: sour grapes, fantasy, delusion. Interesting to listen to; these things are so obvious. But two weren't, and they both had to do with the doctor. These two had the ring of truth to them, and they were similar to each other in some interesting details—some physical things about the doctor—and similar in substance to the dead woman's story as I had been able to piece it together. Quite similar. One of these stories interested me particularly. It was told to me by a beautiful, nervous young woman who was having trouble sustaining relationships. She said that she'd had 'about a thousand of them'—these are her words—and they all ended in about the same way at about the same stage in the development of things. She was getting desperate. She had unresolved issues with a father who had disappeared early in her life, and the doctor offered to help her with this—he, by the way, was just the father's age and, as she herself said, 'talk about missing a red flag.' But anyway, the doctor offered to help her with this in what he called a 'surrogate, therapeutic relationship.' He was candid with her. He said that it was experimental, that he'd never tried it before, but that he was willing to try it with her. And in her words, 'What the heck; what did I have to lose? It was therapy for God's sake.' No anxiety, no guilt, no expectations except that she would get healthy, or healthier. No entanglements. The woman threw herself into it. In fact, she couldn't wait for each session. And she says that for a while it worked; for a while it was—her words—'quite wonderful.'

"Even the sexual part was good. The doctor was a very caring, generous lover. Very gentle. He taught her things about sex. He coached her. He would talk to her as they made love; she would ask questions. Afterward they would analyze what they had done. It was quite clinical and that allowed her to confront her father through him. And that, too, was working; she was just about ready to go see her father for the first time in three years and get some of her feelings out into the open when the unexpected happened. Her father died. Dropped dead out of the blue, and just like that, any chance of dealing with anything was gone.

"She 'came apart,' to use her words again. She immediately called the doctor but—here's the funny part—he didn't return her calls. For three days she called him, paged him, called his emergency number, left messages. No response. Nothing. Nada. She thought it strange. She came to believe that it was the father thing. Somehow the doctor was undone by it, as if it were a message from God or something. In the meantime, she was in distress, so finally, just before Thanksgiving, she went to his office. It was 8:30 in the evening, and his car was still there, although his last appointment was always at 7:00. She waited and waited, and when he didn't come out, she figured he was doing paperwork, so she went in. He had one of those double doors in his waiting room. She knocked, she pushed; it was open. And there he was with a woman, in flagrante delicto. They froze. The doctor was sprawled, the woman was kneeling, our woman was gaping. I asked if there was any chance this might be some kind of therapy. She said that the only therapy going on there was oral therapy, and the patient was administrating it. Our woman screamed. She screamed, 'Paul, you cocksucking, motherfucking sonofabitch!' and then she ran. She slammed the door and ran. That was a long time ago now, and she's never seen or heard from the doctor again. Of course she wouldn't have been easy to find. She disappeared. As she says, she 'left no forwarding address.' She was hospitalized for quite a while. She lost her job and gave up her apartment, got a new cell phone, made everyone she knew swear not to reveal her whereabouts. Still, there's no evidence at all that the doctor ever tried to find her.

"Now here's the interesting thing and the pertinent thing, too, as far as that goes. That night in the doctor's office, our woman not only found out about the other woman, but the other woman found out about her. Our woman has only an impression of the other woman, but I think it is impression enough. She was young, taller than average, thin, had medium-length straight dark hair and dark eyes, and she was Asian.

"The dead woman was a five-foot-six-inch one-hundred-seventeen-pound twenty-eight-year-old Korean. I thought it must have been she, so I was able to check with her insurance company, and sure enough, they were billed for an appointment on that very day, which happened to be sixteen days prior to her death. Can you imagine the doctor actually billing her? Of course, maybe it was just a computer thing that went out automatically, or maybe he realized that to not bill her would be some kind of admission or something. Still . . ." Now the doctor and I sat for some time looking at each other. His breathing was regular. Twice he pursed his lips, probably without realizing he was doing so; once he nearly smiled, and I thought that was intentional.

"Unfortunately," I said, "neither person was willing or felt able to withstand the rigors or publicity of an investigation or trial. I mean, we started the process, we really did. We went to the state licensing board, and they were very interested, but ultimately you have to come forth, you have to testify. And they couldn't do it. So . . ." I left off and looked at him again.

"So . . .," he said. "So, you didn't really have anything at all, did you? If the doctor killed this woman—and that is a very big if—you don't even know how he did it."

"Oh, yes I do. He injected her with morphine. That much I know. And he did it in one of two places, and in one of two ways. That much I also know. He either did it in his office, where she had come drunk and out of control, or he did it in her car. There is an eyewitness who places him in her car on Green Bay Road minutes before her death. *How* is a little less certain. He may have simply jabbed her with a hypodermic needle; she may have been inebriated enough not to notice. Also, we know that he had been giving her large doses of vitamins by injection, and when she came to him drunk, he may have talked her into one of these for some reason or another (to help her sober up?)—it wouldn't have been the first time, and we know she liked these—and then given her morphine instead. Or he could even have done this in the car just before he got out."

Decarre smiled wearily. He looked as if he'd like to go somewhere and take a nap. "So as I said, you didn't really have anything at all, did you?" he said.

"Well, I had all this knowledge, you see, and if no one else was going to do anything with it, clearly it was up to me," I said.

"All right, let's talk about you, then. Where did that leave you?" he asked, carefully minding his tenses.

"Me? Well, I guess at that point I realized I had to kill

the doctor." We looked right into each other's eyes then, for a long time. It was a staring match. I won. Finally his eyes flickered, and just for the briefest moment, they located my backpack on the floor beside me.

Finally he asked, "What do you think would have happened to you had you done so?"

"Okay," I said, "I think I see a pattern to your questions. Let me see how close I am. 'The patient shows a tendency to act or react in the extreme suggesting possible bipolar dysfunction. At the same time he is unrealistic about the consequences of his actions or reactions and seems to be out of touch with reality. To the extent that he feels an inflated sense of moral importance and responsibility, he is somewhat delusional.' How's that? How did I do?"

He smiled at me with those sad eyes of his. "I'm not prepared to make a diagnosis at this time."

I smiled at him. "Actually, I was keenly aware of the possible consequences of my actions. I knew I might get caught. I knew I might spend my life in prison. I knew that there was even a chance my actions would create sympathy for the doctor, overshadow his own sins, maybe even turn him into some kind of martyr. Trouble was, I was even more keenly aware of the consequences of my inaction; he'd continue to practice, he'd probably continue to hurt people, and he might very well kill someone else. I didn't want to spend the rest of my life in prison, of course, but neither did I want to lie awake in bed at night the rest of my life. I didn't want to become one of those sheepish little men you see in the post office or the hardware store who can't look you in the eye. I decided I would have to take the chance. I mean, there are only a few times in life you have to step forward, and this seemed like one of them."

"Was saving the woman another?" He hadn't spoken of her directly before. "Is this compensation?"

"It might have been. I've thought about that, but it doesn't really change things. What mattered was that the doctor be stopped, so I got a gun. Actually, I got two guns because I went back and forth on whether I would shoot him from a distance or at close range. I got a rifle and a pistol. I found a shooting range. I began to develop my skills as a marksman. I became quite good, actually.

"Then I developed a plan." I described my plan in what might have been excruciating detail for Decarre. How I'd located his house on a wooded North Shore ravine near Lake Michigan. How I'd found a perfect place to conceal myself in his neighbor's bushes and yew trees. How I'd been stymied for some time about how to get there and get away because there's no street parking in the neighborhood and the area is heavily patrolled, but how I'd hit on the solution one night waiting for the train when a pack of bikers went by, and I realized that they did not arouse suspicion, they were anonymous and they were quick to disappear into the night on a bike path that ran below ground level and under cross streets most of the way to Evanston. I told him how I'd become a biker, ridden the route a dozen times, timed it, sat in the bushes, watched Decarre and his family, measured their routines and schedules, pulled an imaginary trigger, left an imaginary rifle in the bushes a la Lee Harvey Oswald, ridden away, a minute and a half to the bike trail, twenty-two to Evanston. I said all of this confidentially, as if Decarre were in on the plan, as if he were a coconspirator. By this point in the process his discomfort was evident, and I found myself relishing it.

I continued. "Then one night the gun was real. It was the middle of October. The nights were chilly, the leaves had turned and were starting to fall, and when they had fallen, my cover would be gone. I was running out of time. I knew I had to act. This was the night. I waited and waited. Finally the doctor came out onto this porch, this conservatory they have, all glass, at 9:17. He had a phone in one hand talking on it, a glass of red wine in the other; he sat down on the couch with his back to the window. He sat down and he stayed there. Very cooperative. I fixed his head in my sights. I imagined firing the gun, the glass shattering, the doctor disappearing from view except for a pink spray, a splatter of blood and brain on the wall opposite. I drew a bead on him, and I held it. I held it a long time, but I couldn't shoot him. I just couldn't do it. Finally I put the gun down, took it apart, put it back in the tennis-racket cover I'd brought it in. I just sat there a long time having a talk with myself. It was a soul-searching talk. It was epiphanic. I said to myself, 'Who are you kidding? You're no killer. You can't shoot this guy. You're never going to shoot this guy. You're no killer. You're no cop. You're no private eye. This is all silly.' On my bike ride home, I asked myself the question, 'If you are not those things, then just who are you? Well,' I said to myself, 'I'm a teacher, for one thing. A pretty good teacher, and I'm a writer, and I'm a storyteller.' And then it came to me. That was the answer.

I would tell our story. I would tell our story: my story, your story, Lisa Kim's story, the whole thing." Then I picked up my backpack and held it on my lap.

"And that's what I've done. I've told it. I've written it. It has taken me a long time to do. I actually took a sabbatical to work on it. I spent most of it in a little house in Mexico. I lost one lover and found another. Lots of things changed. My whole life changed, but I did it. I wrote it. Then I sent it out blindly to twenty-five literary agents and one of them, Lorin Rees up in Boston, read it and liked it, and he took it around, and you know what? He found a publisher for it. Tina Pohlman at Harcourt bought it, believe it or not, and you know what else? It was released today. It went on sale this morning all over the country. I stopped in the Lake Forest Book Store on my way here, and there's a whole stack of them sitting right there. Same at Borders. Same at Barnes and Noble. And there's a good chance it's going to be reviewed in the *Tribune* this week if you care to look for it."

Then I unzipped my backpack, took out the book, and put it on the coffee table between us. "And here it is." I turned it 180 degrees so he could read the title. "*Travel Writing*. It's kind of a metaphor. There's a disclaimer, you know the kind, but you'll recognize yourself. Everyone else will recognize you, too." I let him look at it a moment longer; then I flipped open the cover with my index finger. "See, I inscribed it: 'For Lisa.' And see, here it is again in the dedication: 'For Lisa.'"

He stared unblinking at the book, then said almost as if to himself, "None of this really happened."

"Sure it did," I said. "Most of it did. I changed the order

of things; rearranged some things, but you and I both know most of these things really happened."

"Not this conversation," he said.

"Well—"

"How can this conversation be in your book if it's taking place right now?"

"Listen—"

"It never happened, and it never will happen."

"You're right that it hasn't happened, but not that it never will. In some form it's going to happen, and probably in this office."

"But you can't get away with this," he said a bit plaintively. "It's all fabrication."

"No, no. It's not. I *am* going to tell you what I finally have to say. You may hear two minutes of it and throw me out on my ear, or you may hear it all and jab me with a syringe, or you may just read it, but I am going to say this stuff to you one way or another."

"It's slander. That's what it is."

"How much of it you hear and when you hear it I can't control, but it doesn't really matter if you hear it. I mean, the book's in the stores. Whether you hear it or not, you're fucked."

"This is clear-cut libel," he said a little dazed.

"This whole chapter is just for the reader, anyway," I said. "It's a literary device. It's just for the sake of the story. It's Hercule Poirot calling everyone together in the drawing room, you know, or Inspector Morse explaining everything to Sergeant Lewis over a pint of real ale. It's completely unnecessary and—"

"It never happened," he repeated.

"Of course it didn't. That's what we're both saying, isn't it? This part of it never happened. No one is pretending that it did."

"No one's going to believe you, anyway," he said.

"Someone already did. The publisher."

"I'll sue your publisher into bankruptcy," he said, but without much conviction.

"Will you?"

"And I'll sue you for every penny you're worth."

I said, "I think you have to."

"What do you mean?"

"I don't think you have any choice. After all, what if you don't? It will be pretty much an admission of guilt, wouldn't you say?"

"I'll sue you," he said a bit pathetically. "I'll sue you."

"I hope so. You see, apparently we don't have a very strong criminal case, but in a civil court, where the burden of proof is 'preponderance of evidence' and 'reasonable doubt' doesn't apply, we'd win hands down. Then maybe criminal charges can be preferred; who knows what new evidence will come to the fore in a civil case?"

"Like what?" he asked.

"Like this, for instance." I took an envelope from my backpack and held it for him to see. "You know what this is? It's Tanya Kim's sealed, signed, and notarized affidavit."

"*Tanya* Kim?"

"That's right, Tanya Kim. Unfortunately, it can't be un-sealed except in the event of her death or disability; then it's to be turned over to the state's attorney. But that's for now.

282 ... PETER FERRY

She can change her mind; young people often do. She might decide to release this information after she hears the results of the civil case. Wouldn't surprise me at all."

"Do you have any idea how much a lawsuit costs? How are you going to pay for all of this?"

"We intend to sell a few books," I said. "But not this one. This one is complimentary. It's for you." I smiled at him. I zipped my backpack, gathered my jacket, and then stopped in the doorway. "I almost forgot. I believe this was intended for you, too." Then I took Lisa's letter from my hip pocket where I had carried it right between my wallet and me since the day I'd been given it. Time and friction had worn it as smooth and thin as fine silk or polished cotton. I put it on the coffee table beside the book.

"So what happened?" asks Nick.

"What do you mean, 'what happened?'"

"To the guy. The doctor."

"I told you what happened," I say.

"But afterward. Since then. Did he threaten you? Did he run away to Brazil or jump off a bridge or what?" asks the girl whose hair is purple this day.

"There is no 'since then.' I've told you all I know."

"Wait a minute. This is only a story, isn't it?" asks the dog-faced boy.

"It's not only a story," I say, "but it *is* a story."

"I mean, you're just making it up, aren't you?"

"I'm not just making it up, but I *am* making it up," I say.

"What exactly does that mean?" says the dog-faced boy.

"Your coyness is driving me nuts. I want to know what part of this was true. Was there a girl in a car?"

"Yes."

"Was she drunk?"

"Yes."

"Did she crash her car?"

"She did, and I might have been able to stop her, and I was the first one there, and she did change my life, and I did take a sabbatical to write her story."

"You can't just leave it there," says the girl whose hair is purple. "You gotta make the doctor do something."

"No I don't, but I imagine he'll do something."

"Like off himself? Put a bullet through his head?"

"I hope not," I say.

"Do you? Are you sure?" asks Nick. "Don't you want him to die? Don't you want to cause him to die? And how, then, are you different than the doctor wanting Lisa Kim to die?"

"You know, Nick," I say, "you have an uncanny way of hitting the nail on the head. I *do* feel responsible for what happens. That's the trouble with this whole moral-indignation business. Sooner or later you've got to pay the piper. Sooner or later you have to decide if you're really moral or just indignant. It's a lot easier to just be indignant, and I found out that that was most of it for me, but not quite all of it. I also found out that if you're going to call someone else on his morality, you'd better be pretty comfortable with your own."

"And are you?" asks Nick.

"Not comfortable enough," I say. "I've got some work to do."

"But you went ahead anyway," says Nick.

"Yes, I went ahead anyway."

"But where's it go? What's happening in the story right now?" asks the dog-faced boy.

"Well," I say, "I'm sitting here talking to you."

"This is part of the story?"

"It can be."

"You mean we're in the story?"

"If you want to be," I say.

"*I* want to be," says the purple-haired girl.

"Not me," says someone else.

"Cool!" says the dog-faced boy.

"Wait a minute," says Nick. "Does this mean that *that* moment and *this* moment are the same? That the two moments have come together? Like, is the narration now in present tense?"

"Not necessarily," I say.

"Then there's more to tell," says Nick.

"Only if I choose to tell it," I say.

"What do you mean, if you choose to?"

"That's selection," I say, "and selection is what art is, if you want to call this art. Hemingway said that what you leave out is more important than what you put in."

"So what else are you going to put in?" asks the purple-haired girl.

"Nothing," I say. "I think I've said enough."

"What about Lisa Kim? Are you really done with her?"

"I am."

"And is there really a Lydia?" the purple-haired girl goes on.

"No."

"Is there a Carolyn?" she asks.

"Yes."

"Are you seeing Carolyn?"

"Yes."

"What's going to happen there?" asks Nick.

"Don't know. Let's just say we've passed the critical trial period, and we're on an upward trajectory."

"What does that mean?" asks the dog-faced boy.

"They're in love, you dope," says the purple-haired girl.

EPILOGUE

* * *

TRAVEL WRITING

DATELINE: DOOLIN, COUNTY CLARE, IRELAND
by Pete Ferry

CAROLYN WILL SAY it best: "I don't much care where we go, but when we get there, I want to unpack my things and put them in drawers. I want to stay put."

We will have both done the grand tour, bought Eurailpasses, seen seven cities in six days, lugged backpacks, and stood in lines at Internet cafés wondering if there are any Parisians left in Paris. We will have seen London, we will have seen France. Now it will be time to sit somewhere in our underpants with a glass of something and a good book. Besides, it will be our honeymoon.

We will choose Rose Cottage in the village of Doolin in the County of Clare in the West of Ireland. We will find it in the *Self Catering Guide* put out by the Irish Tourist Board.

The great advantage of renting a house is that almost immediately you begin to live there in a way you never do in a hotel room; you buy flowers because you know you're going to outlast them; you concern yourself with toilet paper and bathtub rings; you rearrange the furniture; you stock the fridge.

You become, however briefly, a member of a nontransient community and, as is always the case when you live in a place, your ultimate impression is much different than your initial one.

That will be good in the case of Rose Cottage. Actually our *very* first impression will be quite positive. When we'll turn into the yard just off the high road to the Cliffs of Moher, we'll be a little thrilled. A hundred-year-old house on a working farm, Rose Cottage will have a high, peaked roof of thatching, three-foot-thick whitewashed walls, bright blue shutters, and window boxes of colorful impatiens.

But the thick walls and small windows will make the common room dark, the beds will sag, the kitchen will be somewhere between utilitarian and drab, and the only view of the rolling green land, blue sea, and Aran Islands to the west will be from the bathroom because a large metal barn completely lacking in the kind of charm Americans go to Europe for will block all other windows.

The place will have been thrown wide open all lights ablaze, radio blaring, and peat burning in the fireplace. We will poke about trying not to be disappointed. "Bedrooms are cute," we'll say. "It's got a shower."

Suddenly Breda Logan will dash in out of the drizzle wiping her hands on her apron. "Raining," she'll say. "Now here's this and here's that. Blankets in the cupboard, and I've brought you a load of peat for the fire. More behind the barn if you need it. No time to chat you up right now. Cakes in me oven. Back soon." It will be the last we'll see of her until the very hour of our departure two weeks later.

"Before you go, could you show us where Doolin is?"

"Well, just there," she'll say with a broad wave of her arm as we cross the yard toward the pasture.

"Where?"

"Just there," she'll say, a tiny bit frustrated, but all we'll see will be a scattering of farmhouses along a road far below us, nothing that resembles a village much less a town, certainly not the traditional music capital of all Ireland.

But it will be Doolin, okay, although when we'll get up close we'll find some more of it hidden beneath the lip of the hill. Still, it won't be much: one pub and a handful of shops at one end of the road, two more and a few houses half a mile away at the other, a few B&Bs and a small hotel or two in between, a tiny yellow church just recently built on a bare hilltop, looking as if it belongs in Montana.

We'll walk the road for an hour and then pass campgrounds on our way down to the water's edge. We'll have a pint and some okay fish chowder in one of the pubs and listen to some music that won't be as good as the townie band we'll have heard in Clifton the night before. We'll give up and go home to bed.

The morning forecast will be for brighter weather, but it will still be wet and cool when we get up. Fourth of July mass and we'll stand at the back with several ruddy-faced, fidgety men looking the worse for last night's wear. The priest's homily will be about being nice to Americans; "Hardly a soul in Doolin doesn't have someone in the States, I should think."

Outside a car will stop and an Italian man will ask directions in broken English, and I will start to say I don't know, but then I'll realize that I do. He'll have asked about the one place whose location I'll happen to know. Left at the corner, two kilometers, left at the police station, straight on.

We'll sack two tiny grocery stores in nearby Lisdoonvarna for picnic stuff and makings for a dinner Carolyn will want to cook, and by noon there will be a bowl of fruit on the kitchen table, fresh-cut flowers on the mantel, and tunes in the air.

I will find a mackintosh hanging in the hallway and some wellies and set about cleaning and moving some lawn furniture I'll find down behind the barn to an open space where our glasses will be able to sit on the stone wall, our feet to rest on the pasture gate, and we to look over the backs of the cows through the fog to where the sea and Aran Isles will be alleged to be. Coming back around I will be surprised to see a tour bus stopped in the road and lots of Japanese faces behind Japanese cameras taking lots of pictures. Most of the cameras will be aimed at Rose Cottage, but as the bus will slowly move away, a couple will swivel to snap me. I'll tip my cap and try to think of something Pat O'Brien–ish to say. One day we'll be strangers in a strange land; the next we'll damn near be natives.

By noon we'll be off on the five-mile hike to the dramatic Cliffs of Moher that fall away a thousand feet into the sea. We'll have lunch in our backpack and hope in our hearts that the drizzle will be just a heavy mist. At first we'll walk farmers' lanes for some time just one step ahead of a herd of cows being moved from pasture to pasture by some farm boys, but halfway there we'll find ourselves back on the main road alongside fast cars and fumey tour buses.

Then it will rain. We'll seek shelter in an animal pen beside the road and as we'll wait out the shower, we'll watch a couple coming down through the fields from what will look like the cliffs. When they reach us, we'll ask if we'll be able to get to the visitor center that way.

"Yes, but don't go. There are fifty thousand people there. Just climb up the path a bit for the best view of the cliffs." Half an hour later, we'll be having Stilton cheese, crusty bread, ham, apples, and wine, practically dangling our feet over the cliff. The sun will be out and strong and we'll be down to our T-shirts.

Will there ever be a lovelier place or moment in the world? We'll laugh aloud. We'll sing John Prine's lyric: "Half an inch of water and you think you're going to drown, that's the way that the world goes round."

We'll watch a lone hiker coming up the cliff path from Doolin and offer him a glass of wine when he gets to us. Yes, you can come all the way, he'll assure us, so we'll go all the way back to town climbing over stone walls and holding barbed wire apart for each other, turning often for head-shaking views of the cliffs. In five miles we'll meet just six people.

Then I'll be back at Rose Cottage sitting with my feet on the gate, and the Aran Islands will have magically appeared one after another in the bright blue world beyond me. I'll be able to hear Carolyn's clatter and music in the kitchen, and soon she'll join me for a pint of Guinness and the sunset. Afterward we'll build a peat fire and eat Carolyn's wonderful chicken, ham, and leek pie in front of it. Very Irish. It is always nice to make a small home in a far place.

Ten days later, we'll take the hour-long ferry ride to Inishmore, the largest and most distant of the Aran Islands, last refuge of Celtic culture and the very edge of Europe, next stop Boston. We'll spend the day riding bikes through the endless labyrinth of stone-walled farm lanes, chatting with students at an archeological dig, crawling on our bellies to the edge of a three hundred–foot drop at the fortress called Dun Aengus, which dates to 2000 B.C., overhearing schoolboys in uniform arguing in Gaelic.

Then we'll be having pints and sandwiches at a picnic table in a sunny beer garden at the top of the village when Jon and Cynthia Lynch will come along. "Mind?"

"Not at all." They will have just arrived and be poring over their guidebooks.

"Do you know if you can rent bikes in Doolin?" they'll ask.

"Yes," we'll say, "there are two places right in the main road."

"And where do you ride?"

We'll tell them about the coastal road that we'll have ridden to a manor house cum hotel called Aran View House, and the good dinner we'll have eaten there. We'll tell them about riding back away from the sea into the rocky landscape called the Burren, about the fifteenth-century, five-story-tall shell of a castle called Lemeneagh that we'll have trespassed on a working farm to tour because there'll be no one around to guide us or even charge us a fee, and about the ruined village that surrounds it outlined in tumbled-down stone walls; we'll tell them about Carron Church, another fifteenth-century ruin, very quiet and just sitting in someone's field. And Portal Dolmen, a tiny stone shelter 3,500 years old, the oldest constructed habitation known on earth, where a farmer sitting in his car will have taken a donation in a plastic bucket and then disappeared, we'll imagine, to the nearest pub.

"Is the hotel the best restaurant?"

We'll say that we liked Branoch na n Aille, an old stone house right in the village, with plank floors, plain furniture, and wonderful food.

"How about the pubs?"

"McGann's has a good feel and good food," Carolyn will say, "but the music seemed a bit more casual. We heard the best musicians at McDermotts, but we ate wonderful mussels outside at a picnic table at McGann's."

Back on the mainland we'll read books on the grassy banks above the little harbor, then walk the two miles back to Rose Cottage for the last time, drink a Guinnesss with the last sunset, our feet on the pasture gate, cook a last meal of Guinness stew full of meat, carrots, and prunes, warm ourselves at our last peat fire.

In the morning we'll be packed and ready when Tom and Breda Logan will bound into our living room like vaudevillians onto a stage. They'll clap and laugh and bluster. "And it's been a fine holiday now, has it?" she'll say.

"I should say. Been going by on me tractor, and those bedroom curtains are always drawn."

"So it's your honeymoon, then, is it?" she'll say.

"And not his first from the look of him, I shouldn't think," he'll say.

I'll laugh.

"Only married four years meself. Bachelor all me days till the age of forty, then I met Breda here and—"

"Wham!" she'll say. "Nothing but bliss since." They'll eye each other, laugh in unison, and slap their thighs.

"Grew up in this house, lived here, and farmed the land till Breda says, 'Let's build the new one cross the way and let this one to holidayers.'"

"But you still farm the land?" Carolyn will ask.

"I do, and in the fields sixteen hours a day this time of year."

"And what do you do in the States?" Breda will ask.

"I'm an attorney," Carolyn will say.

"I'm a teacher," I'll say, "and a writer. I write travel stories."

"Oh, really? For newspapers, then? And what do you write about?"

"Oh, just the places we go, the people we meet."

"Local color and all of that?" he'll say. "So are you going to write about Doolin?"

"I think I might," I'll say.

"Now, don't be putting us in there as your local color," she'll say.

"Okay, I won't."

"Or if you do," he'll say, "don't be telling the truth."